SCHOOLS COUNCIL EXAMINATIONS BULLETIN 32

Assessment and testing in the secondary school

R. N. Deale
Central Examinations Research and Development Unit
Schools Council

Foreword by JACK WRIGLEY
University of Reading

Evans/Methuen Educational

*First published 1975 for the Schools Council
by Evans Brothers Limited
Montague House, Russell Square, London WC1B 5BX
and Methuen Educational Limited
11 New Fetter Lane, London EC4P 4EE*

*Distributed in the US by Citation Press
Scholastic Magazines Inc., 50 West 44th Street
New York, NY 10036
and in Canada by Scholastic–TAB Publications Ltd
123 Newkirk Road
Richmond Hill, Ontario*

© *Schools Council Publications 1975*

ISBN 0 423 50260 3

*Printed in Great Britain by
Richard Clay (The Chaucer Press) Ltd
Bungay, Suffolk*

Assessment and testing
in the secondary school

Contents

Acknowledgements

The Schools Council and the publishers are grateful to the Associated Lancashire Schools Examining Board for permission to reproduce their May 1974 CSE English/Paper I (Written Expression); to Hubert Nicholson for the A. S. J. Tessimond poem 'A Hot Day', in question A1 of that examination paper, and to Penguin Books Ltd for the extract from the Edwin Brock poem 'Five Ways to Kill a Man' (from *Penguin Modern Poets No. 8*), in question A4. The photograph for use with question B5 is reproduced by courtesy of A. F. Kersting from M. Webb's *Architecture in Britain Today* (Country Life Books, 1969); that for use with question B6(a) by courtesy of the Science Museum, South Kensington, London, from C. F. Caunter's *The Light Car* (HMSO, 1970); that for use with question B7(b) by courtesy of the Victoria & Albert Museum, South Kensington, London, from J. P. Hartham's *Bookbindings* (HMSO, 1961), and that for use with question C10 by courtesy of the City Planning Officer of the City of Liverpool from M. Dower's *The Challenge of Leisure* (Civic Trust, 1965).

Thanks are also expressed to J. K. Backhouse (University of Oxford), to J. Miller (Blakelaw School, Newcastle upon Tyne) and to G. F. Peaker (formerly of HM Inspectorate) for the examples of methods of assessment and analysis which they have contributed in Chapters IV, V and VI.

Foreword

In 1972 the Schools Council was at an early stage in its work on the possible reform of the public examination system. A group of staff in the Central Examinations Research and Development Unit (CERDU) and a key committee, the Joint Examinations Sub-committee (JESC), decided to produce a straightforward, practical book on assessment for teachers. This examinations bulletin is the result. Commissioned by JESC, the book is the responsibility of CERDU, but the main credit must go to the author, R. N. Deale. There are two main difficulties encountered in the attempt to write a simple account of assessment procedures. The first is to avoid making false statements when writing in an elementary manner, the second is to avoid a patronizing tone. All the members of the Schools Council committees who have read this book share my view that Rory Deale has made a difficult task seem easy, and has been remarkably successful in responding to his brief.

The Schools Council, together with its predecessors the Secondary School Examinations Council and the Curriculum Study Group, has now produced thirty-two examinations bulletins in a series which has made a considerable contribution to knowledge and understanding about assessment and examination issues. In many ways this examinations bulletin is a natural successor to Examinations Bulletin No. 1, *The Certificate of Secondary Education: Some Suggestions for Teachers and Examiners*, a book produced when CSE was being planned. The first bulletin is still well worth reading – it has a good deal to say about the principles of examining and illustrates those principles from the point of view of the individual subjects of the curriculum. But as regards assessment in the classroom, Examinations Bulletin No. 1 dealt essentially with general principles and there has always been a need for a more detailed treatment of the ideas put forward. This bulletin by Rory Deale provides this detailed treatment.

Three main strands have run through the examinations bulletin series. The first is concerned with the development of better public examination procedures, the second with research into the methods of examining and the third with the better use of assessment techniques and procedures by teachers. All three themes are important, but it is the last which is exemplified in this book. It continues a theme begun in 1963 with Examinations Bulletin No. 1, continued in Examinations Bulletin No. 5, *The Certificate of Secondary Education: School-based Examinations: Examining, Assessing and Moderating by Teachers* (1965), in Examinations Bulletin 27, *Assessment of Attainment in Sixth-form Science* (1973)

9

and in Examinations Bulletin 31, *Continuous Assessment in the CSE: Opinion and Practice* (1975).

By the time this book is published I shall have ended my long association with the Council. As I look back on my work on the examinations front I believe that I shall be most pleased to have been associated with Examinations Bulletins 1 and 32, the first and last (to date) in the series. Both exemplify my own personal beliefs that teaching and examining should be considered together, that the knowledge needed to understand assessment techniques is not great, although important, and that teachers are quite capable of handling the techniques required. Most of the knowledge needed is described in this examinations bulletin.

JACK WRIGLEY
Professor of Curriculum Research and Development
University of Reading
and Director of Studies, Schools Council (1967–75)

Preface

Assessment, testing, examining – these are topics which many people tend to regard with somewhat mixed feelings. Some may dismiss them as abstractions which bear little relation to the practical problems of teaching, while others see them as involving mathematical complexities such that they are beyond the comprehension of ordinary beings.

It must be admitted that there can be a certain amount of justification for such views; it *is* possible to make a life's work out of a study of the theory and the practice of mental measurement and, unfortunately, many of the published works of those who have done so are written in a language so obscure as to be comprehensible only to fellow devotees.

Nevertheless, the basic principles are not difficult to understand and it is not necessary to be a mathematician to do so; the principles are applicable to all subjects and an understanding of them is important to all teachers. The only 'mathematical' activities required are counting, adding up and subtracting, plus the ability to work out a percentage – the calculations used beyond these become so tedious that nowadays they are left to a computer and in any case are worth doing only when the numbers involved run into many times those in any individual school.

In this book we are concerned with the situation confronting the class teacher who needs to make assessments of his or her pupils for a variety of purposes, perhaps to meet the internal requirements of the school, or to help to make the teaching more effective, or as part of the procedures of an external examination. We have avoided lengthy theoretical discussions and tried to keep to a strictly practical level. Suggestions for additional reading are given at the end of each chapter for those who wish to investigate further.

To some extent, we must ask the reader to exercise a little charity; we have drawn examples from as many different subjects as possible but in order to make them intelligible to non-specialists we have had to keep to what subject teachers may think is an absurdly naïve level. Ideally, we should have liked to write a different version of this book for every subject; we would therefore ask for tolerance from the subject specialist, and ask that he should bear with weaker brethren who are here afforded just a glimpse of the less esoteric mysteries of his own discipline.

Within these limitations, it is hoped that this book will be of some use in its own right as a guide through a rather complex jungle, in which there are numerous false trails and pitfalls for the unwary, and serve also as an introduction to a study of what can be an interesting and important aspect of teaching.

Thanks must be expressed to past and present colleagues in CERDU – Dr G. Barratt, Dr L. Cohen, J. A. Everson, Dr D. L. Nuttall, A. C. Reid, C. H. Smith, G. S. Bardell and E. O. James – whose comments and suggestions have improved early drafts beyond measure. Responsibility for the shortcomings that remain must be my own.

R.N.D.

I. General principles – types of test – terms and definitions

In this introductory chapter, we shall take some examples and discuss the four main types of test appropriate to different school situations and the various reasons why teachers need to make assessments. We shall look at some of the principles of test construction and define some terms used in the rest of the book.

Testing in schools – some examples and principles

EXAMPLE 1

> With his first-year groups in an unstreamed comprehensive school, a science teacher finds that he must spend some time teaching the children the names and functions of the laboratory equipment before he can start practical work. When he has completed this part of his programme, he needs to find out if his teaching has been effective.

We are here concerned with the type of assessment known as *mastery testing*; the aim is to discover whether all the children know enough – have mastered the topic well enough – to start on the next stage of the course. The term testing should not be taken to mean exclusively a formal written test; there are many test techniques available and, in Example 1, it would be reasonable to adopt a quick and informal method, such as oral question-and-answer around the class.

The first principle (and a very important one) to be considered is that of *fitness-for-purpose*. The test should be devised with a specific aim in view. If there are confused or conflicting aims, the test cannot be expected to perform efficiently and its results may be dangerously misleading.

Once the aim of the test is established, the test technique chosen should be suitable for the purpose intended. In our example, it would not be appropriate to point out the equipment and to ask the children to write down what it is used for; to score well on such a test, they would certainly have to know about the equipment but also to possess the ability to give a written description of its function. Since the teacher wants only to find out whether or not the children are ready to start the practical work, he should choose a testing method which will not confuse the results by introducing another factor. For example, he could ask the children to name or point out the equipment which is needed for a certain experiment, the experiment being described by him, not by the children.

13

The results of a mastery test should show a lot of top marks, with perhaps a short tail of those near the top, indicating that the class as a whole has a reasonably good understanding of the topic. If the marks do not come out like this, *either* the class has not learned enough *or* the test was a bad one.

This last possibility must always be borne in mind and the science teacher, if in doubt, should check the results by letting some of the low-scorers use the equipment in practice to see what happens – under supervision. However, if he has used his test satisfactorily in previous years, he should be reasonably sure about how well it works and how to interpret its results.

This brings us to another important point: a good test is hard to make, and if you have a good one – one that works well in practice and gives you the information you need – it is worth while keeping it to use again. But it must be remembered that if the syllabus has changed, the test may no longer be appropriate and it would be putting the cart before the horse to keep the same syllabus just because you have some good tests.

The test must be devised to suit the teaching situation, not the reverse.

EXAMPLE 2

A school offers its pupils the opportunity of starting to learn German in the second year. In recommending to parents whether or not this opportunity should be accepted, the headteacher studies the summer exam results and tells the parents that the children should start learning German only if they have scored over 50 per cent in the French exam. Is this a justifiable procedure?

The answer is probably not, certainly not in such definite terms. It is likely that if children have done well at French they have an aptitude for learning languages and the chances are that they will be good at German but, to be as positive as the headteacher is in the example, he would have to prove two things:

i   that *all* children who had got more than 50 per cent in French always did well at German;
ii that *no* children who got less than 50 per cent ever did well.

It is unlikely that either of these could be done, because no examination can be that precise.

The problem arises because the headteacher is trying to use the French exam for a purpose it was not intended for. He is using it as a *predictive* or *aptitude test* to estimate the future success of children on a new course. The French exam was probably designed as a *discriminating attainment test,* that is, one that attempts to distinguish different levels of attainment as clearly as possible.

14

Most school examinations are designed as discriminating attainment tests, to provide information on children's progress and standards of work, as are most public examinations, which have to distinguish passes from fails, grade 1s from grade 2s, etc. Results of a discriminating test should show marks well spaced out; a lot of ties or a lot of candidates bunched together would indicate that it has not done the job it was meant to do.

Predictive or aptitude tests are much less common in schools, though widely used in the United States and, recently, in personnel selection in this country. The most familiar example of a predictive test is the 11+ examination which attempts to identify those children who will benefit from an academic secondary education.

Considerable doubt has been cast on the ability of the 11+ or any predictive test to forecast attainment with the degree of accuracy required. Certainly, many people nowadays would claim that it is almost impossible to identify the complex factors involved in the subsequent success, or otherwise, of children who have been selected for different types of secondary school. The fact of having 'passed' or 'failed' the examination at 11 almost certainly contributes to raising or depressing later achievements; thus the very prediction of success or failure may itself be an important factor in bringing about the predicted result.

Whatever the merits or demerits of predictive tests, the French exam in Example 2 is certainly not intended to be one and the assumption that its results can be used in this way is not justifiable unless there is a lot of hard evidence to back it up. The headteacher should certainly refer to the French results, for the reason given above, but he should also take many other factors into consideration – marks in other subjects, interest and motivation, attitude to work and the results of his recommendations in previous years – before advising parents.

EXAMPLE 3

The teacher in charge of a remedial English class introduces a new reading scheme and after a year wants to check on the progress made.

The purpose of the teacher here is twofold; he is concerned with the reading progress of his class and, from this, to make an evaluation of the new scheme. In this case a discriminating attainment test would be appropriate and there are three possibilities open to the teacher:

i   to use the questions and exercises at the back of the reading book as a test;
ii   to use a standardized reading test;
iii to use his own test.

If he chooses **i** the results may show how well his pupils have progressed on the particular scheme, relative to one another. They will not show him how well they have progressed relative to last year's pupils or to reading standards in general.

If he chooses **ii** he will certainly gain some information about his pupils' general reading standards, and if he used the same test last year, with a similar group, he will be able to find out something about the value of the new scheme compared with the old one.

If he chooses **iii** he may, or may not, gain a similar amount of information, depending on how well he has designed the test, whether he used it last year or not and how suitable it is to the new course.

A *standardized test* seems likely, therefore, to be the most useful in this situation. This is a test which has been designed to measure some particular aspect of attainment, personality, intelligence, etc. Standardized means that the test has been widely tried out under carefully controlled conditions and the scores analysed so that the results of an individual on the test can be related to some 'normal' or 'average' figure. Thus, a standardized reading test will usually offer a way of converting the scores into a 'reading age' which means the average age at which a certain score can be reached. A score of, say, 55 on the test might be converted into a reading age of 10, which means that the 'average' 10-year-old will score 55; if a 13-year-old in the remedial class gets the same score, then he is three years later than the average in reaching this level of reading skill.*

Standardized tests take a long time to make because the test has to be given to a large number of people in order to work out the norms; the test will usually have to be revised several times and much analysis has to be done to make sure that it gives rise to stable and consistent scores. Once the test has been completed, it is a major task to alter it and so it tends to remain unchanged for a number of years. It is important, also, to administer the test always under the same conditions as any changes, such as using typed copies of the test paper rather than the printed form, can invalidate its results.

It may seem contradictory, therefore, to recommend the use of a standardized test in view of what has previously been said about the test being devised to suit the teaching situation, but it is again a question of fitness-for-purpose. The teacher of the remedial class in Example 3 is concerned with the development of reading skill in his pupils, not with knowledge of the content of the books used, though understanding the texts is a necessary step in his programme of work. He uses the books as a means of developing reading ability to the end of

* If two different standardized tests are given, it will almost certainly be found that the results are different, though the variations may be quite small. This is caused by the inevitable inaccuracy of any test and variations in pupils' performances from day to day. As we said before, *no* test can be expected to be 100 per cent accurate.

improving the general level of competence of his pupils, so that they can read not just the course books, but newspapers, magazines, etc. as well. He needs, therefore, a measure of this general reading ability and the best measure will probably be a test devised and standardized in the manner outlined above. If he makes his own test, he will know very little about how its results relate to any standards outside his own school, or possibly even outside his own class, and the results will be of less value.

There are tests available of social adaptation, of personality, prognostic tests such as those which attempt to predict the likelihood of delinquency and many others which come into the specialized province of the psychologist and are outside the scope of this book. In the school situation, there are obviously many other occasions on which a standardized attainment test could be useful, since it could provide valuable information on standards within one school compared with others, but unfortunately there are not many available at present and those which do exist are mainly concerned with attainment in literacy and numeracy.*

There are signs, however, that the situation may be changing; standardized attainment tests are widely used (perhaps too widely used) in the United States and it would be as well to give a warning about some of the dangers. The standardized reading test, which we have taken as our example, is a test of reading skill, not of content, which, in this instance, is immaterial. Where the content of the test is important (which is the case with the majority of school subjects) there is a serious risk either that the test will be unsuitable for use in many schools because of different syllabuses or that the school's syllabus will be constrained in order to fit the test.

We make no apology for repeating what we regard as the first commandment: the test must be devised to suit the teaching situation. However, this can be modified a little by saying devised or chosen because, as we have seen, there can be reasons for choosing a ready-made test, provided that the choice is made with great care. If a suitable standardized test is chosen, then it must be used with discretion. In our example, the value of the test would be completely negated if the teacher started to teach his pupils how to get a good mark on this test. This could easily be done: he could list the words used in the test and get his class to learn them by heart. They would then score high marks – falsely high, because they would have learned only those few words and might still be quite incapable of reading any others.

---

* Standardized attainment tests should not be confused with multiple-choice (objective) questions, in different subjects, which are now on the market. These multiple-choice questions have often not been pre-tested or validated in any way; a standardized test, on the other hand, is accompanied by a test manual which gives full details of the test's design and development, the pupils for whom it is suitable, instructions for its administration and information on the analysis and interpretation of its results.

The value of the test lies in the fact that the words used in it have been found in practice to be a fair sample of the words people need to know. There is a good chance,* therefore, that the number of test words that somebody gets right will correspond roughly to the total number of words he knows, or, in other words, to his general reading ability. But obviously, this does not mean that if only the particular sample of words in the test are taught, then automatically all the others are known.

The great danger in the use of standardized tests lies in this fact: it is possible to distort the results by deliberately teaching for the test. If the test is used by the teacher for the purpose it was intended for (that is, to measure attainment at some stage in the teacher's programme of work) there is no problem. The risk lies in the temptation to alter the programme to suit the test; this risk is much greater where such tests are used in external examinations (in Sweden, for example), and for this reason examining boards in the United Kingdom are very careful to consider the 'backwash' effect of their examinations on the schools. The backwash effect must also be remembered even when considering internal tests and examinations in an individual school: the test procedure should not adversely affect the teaching nor should it ever be necessary to teach in a particular way, or to concentrate on a particular topic, simply in order to score well on a test.

The question of backwash applies, of course, to all tests and examinations, not just to standardized tests. Backwash can be beneficial: the increased weighting given to oral tests and the introduction of tests of listening comprehension in many public examinations have certainly encouraged teachers of modern languages to give more attention to oral/aural work in their schools.

Backwash from a standardized test, however, is likely to be adverse, since the test will probably be restricted in content and, if misused, may encourage a very narrow approach. This is one reason (though by no means the only one) why examining boards use a wide variety of testing techniques – essay, objective test, practical, etc. – to ensure that teachers are encouraged to adopt a broad approach to their subject. The teacher using a standardized test in school must make a conscious effort not to let it influence his teaching.

There is one other type of test worth mentioning – the *diagnostic test*. Diagnostic tests are aimed at finding out the causes of learning difficulties which may be due to some serious psychological deficiency such as the inability to distinguish the characteristic shapes of letters and figures. This is probably a type of test which is best left to the educational psychologist, but at a less fundamental level, diagnostic attainment tests are available to help the teacher concerned with lack of progress in literacy and numeracy.

There can, of course, be a diagnostic or predictive element in any test; for

* The word chance is used deliberately; probabilities can be calculated and a standardized test should give an estimate of the likely error in the scores.

example, a score of 0 on a mastery test shows clearly enough that the material has not been learned. Consistently low marks in, say, mathematics, physics and chemistry indicate that a pupil is not likely to do well in the science sixth form. Information of this kind can be obtained from tests which are not specifically designed for the purpose of diagnosis or prediction – they can certainly show that the problems are there, and they may provide an indication of aptitude, though they should not be too rigidly interpreted in this way.

Why assess?

We have considered some examples of tests being used in schools for a number of purposes; we should now try to summarize the reasons why the teacher needs to make assessments of his pupils.

Feedback

The teacher needs to make assessments in order to help him teach more efficiently – he needs feedback. He needs to find out if what has been taught has been learned. He needs to know whether or not the pupils have understood the work properly so that misconceptions can be corrected. If one piece of knowledge or understanding of a particular idea is an essential first building block before a second can be learned and understood, then the teacher must make sure that each pupil has acquired it before moving on to the next stage. The teacher also must have means of finding out whether his approach to a particular topic was successful or whether he has to try again with a different method. He must be able to gauge his pupils' level of attainment and ability if he is to direct them to the next stage. And he must have feedback to enable him to adjust the pace of his course – not so fast that the children are left floundering, nor so slow that one topic is taught to exhaustion-point and the rest of the course suffers.

Monitoring progress

The teacher needs to monitor the progress of individuals or classes. Pupils may have to be allocated to different streams or sets, and their levels of attainment in the particular subject(s) concerned are usually important factors in these decisions. Progress of parallel sets under different teachers may need to be compared; checks must be made on the progress of individual pupils in a class (particularly in mixed-ability groups) if the teacher is to know who may need extra help. A teacher new to a school or to a particular group may find records of previous attainments helpful to him in becoming acquainted with his pupils. Parents (and pupils) will want to know what progress is being made from year to year and what standards have been reached.

19

Evaluation of materials

The teacher may have to compare new teaching materials with old. Schools can be involved in heavy expenses for textbooks and other materials. Plenty of people are ready to tell teachers that this method or that book solves all the problems of teaching a particular subject. Does it? Do the children learn more, or learn more quickly, or like learning more than with the old method or the old book? It is necessary to have something to base judgements on – how well *did* they do last year? Are they further ahead this year? Is it a better class or are the teaching aims of the new course different, so that direct comparisons are not possible?

Aid to learning

The testing situation can also be an aid to learning. It can be an incentive to the pupils, a goal to aim for and a focus for a course of study. Children like to know how well they have done; and a test soon after material has been learned, by giving the children an opportunity to reuse the material, can help them to remember it better.*

But there are dangers here. Over-use of the 'test-as-a-goal' can lead to the worst sort of exam cramming, to a neglect of those aspects of the course which are not tested or not testable, and it can stimulate an unhealthy competitiveness in the school. It is not reasonable to expect a child to survive unscathed an educational experience which repeatedly points out his inadequacy and it is unwise, therefore, to give too much emphasis to tests which must place someone at the bottom of the list – particularly if it is always the same someone. And there are other ways of reusing recently learned material without always having to set a test on it.

Information on attainments

Records of school attainments are important to those outside the school. We have mentioned the need for keeping parents (and pupils) informed about school progress. Employers, too, will usually want to have some sort of guide, in the form of examination certificates or school references, etc. to the attainments of young people looking for jobs. Entry to higher education, also, may be dependent on the satisfactory completion of the secondary stage. It is part of a teacher's responsibility to make sure that this information is available to assist his pupils in their future careers.

Teaching and assessing

We have seen that there are serious arguments for considering assessment as a necessary part of teaching and, as a result, there can be serious consequences if

---

* See, for example, Ian M. L. Hunter, *Memory* (Penguin Books, 1964).

20

the assessment is inaccurate. A child placed, for example, in the wrong stream (either too high or too low) may suffer a loss of confidence which can mean that he never develops his abilities to the full. Careers guidance may be based in part on success or failure in some subject area and again an error could have long-term effects on the pupil's adult life. Nor can this part of a teacher's responsibility be entirely delegated to an external examining body. The very decision on which pupils ought to be entered for public examinations and in which subjects will to a large extent depend on the teacher's own assessment of the pupils' capabilities. Education is concerned with children's development – with the development of personality, skills, abilities. If the teacher is taking his job seriously, he ought to know the current state of development of the children in his charge and to do this he needs to be equipped with a variety of techniques to make his assessments and to record and interpret the results.

We recognize that there is a view that it is not part of a teacher's function to make any assessments at all and that nothing is gained by placing pupils in a rank order; some would go further and say that in certain subject areas (mainly concerned with the creative arts) it is neither possible nor meaningful to attempt to do so.

It should be remembered that not all tests produce a rank order (the mastery test is one that does not) and that in other cases the rank order is unimportant, for example, in providing feedback, or in a diagnostic test.

Nevertheless, a discriminating test is intended to produce a rank order – this is its purpose – and we have a certain amount of sympathy with the view that this is a sort of egg-grading process which, in certain cases, may be inappropriate, particularly where some creative work is concerned.

Ideally, the assessment should be made in relation to each child's potential, how far each has made use of his ability, rather than in competition with his peers. But we are very far from the ideal, and the measurement of potential is an area where techniques are even less accurate than in the measurement of attainment. As teachers, we may often have a feeling that a certain child could work harder, or that another has done his best even though his results are not very good. If we are honest with ourselves, we will realize how often we are wrong and recognize that there are serious dangers that a first impression, say, of dullness, could affect one's judgement for a long time and lead to a child's never being expected to rise above mediocrity. Furthermore, it can be misleading to both pupil and parents if they are told that the child has worked very well, to the best of his ability, all through the school, only to find at the end of the course that he has attained no more than a very modest level indeed.

So we would advocate a combination of the two approaches: estimates of achievement in relation to potential, together with as objective an assessment of that achievement as possible. We recognize the limitations of our assessment techniques only too well and we would claim no more than that they can provide a basis on which judgements can be made. Much still depends on the teacher's interpretation of results.

In this book, we are attempting to equip teachers with knowledge of the appropriate test techniques but ultimately it is for the individual to decide how to use them.

Definition of terms

Before going any further into the elements of test design, it is necessary to define what we mean by the word 'test' and the closely related terms 'assessment' and 'examination'.

Assessment is used in this book as an all-embracing term, covering any of the situations in which some aspect of a pupil's education is, in some sense, measured by the teacher, or another person. Thus, a comment on a child's general attitude to his school work, for the purpose of an end-of-term report, is based on an assessment in this sense. A mark for a piece of homework is also an assessment, as are the marks on classroom tests. And a public examination, too, makes an assessment of the candidate's attainment.

A *test* refers to a particular situation set up for the purpose of making an assessment. The pencil-and-paper test in the classroom is an obvious example but an essay subject set for homework or classwork also provides a test situation, though this may not be its only function.

Examination refers to a larger scale test, or, more commonly, a combination of several tests, and perhaps other assessment procedures, whether within the school or conducted by an external examining board. An examination in French, for example, may include a test of translation, a composition test, an oral test and perhaps an objective test of comprehension as well, thus attempting to measure attainment in several different aspects of the subject. If it is an external examination, it may be that the oral test is carried out in the school by the teacher while the other tests, with written answers, are sent away to be marked; in some cases, also, the teacher may be asked to contribute an assessment of course work to be taken into account with the results of the other tests in awarding the final grade.

We would not, therefore, see any sharp distinction between the three terms but a considerable overlap. 'Continuous' assessment, for example, may be based on a series of tests (or mini-examinations) at the end of each unit of a course, or be a succession of periodical reviews of work done in class or at home, taking into account oral contributions to class discussions, private study or investigations, practical work, and so on. We would argue that all these are variations on the same theme and that the same principles should underly the construction of a

22

standardized test, an examination or a classroom test though there will be important differences in degree and detail.

In this book we are concerned primarily with the assessment of attainment though we shall touch on the difficult topic of the assessment of attitudes later. The whole range of testing situations between formal (that is the most rigidly structured) and informal is illustrated in Figure 1. The standardized test, as we

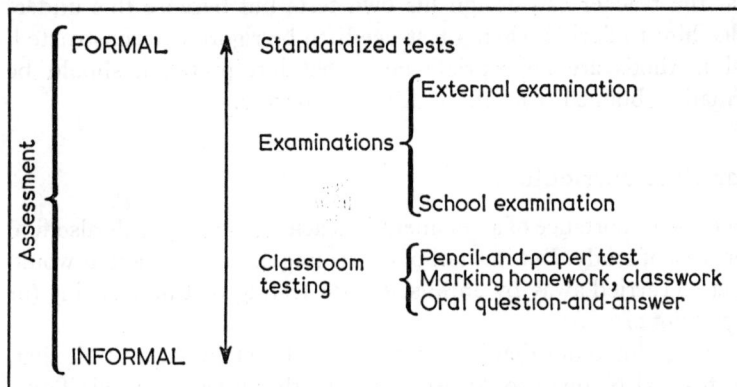

Fig. 1 Range of testing techniques for assessment of attainment

have seen, represents the most formal end of the spectrum, with conditions of administration etc. rigidly laid down. At the other extreme, the 'pure' testing situation is intermingled with teaching/learning aims as well; the teacher asking questions in class about the book the children have read is not only conducting an informal mastery test to make sure they have understood it but is also seeking to awaken their interest, to stimulate their response, and to clarify obscure points for pupils who have not completely grasped them as well as providing himself with feedback on the suitability of the text and the children's reactions to it.

Similarly, the essay set for homework provides a test situation but also has an important teaching function by allowing the children to practise writing skills, to reuse what they have learned and to apply their knowledge and skills to a new topic.

At this end of the spectrum, therefore, the testing aspect may not be of paramount importance; it may in fact be only a very minor part and therefore considerations of reliability and validity etc. which are dealt with in the next chapter may not need to be accorded the weight which should be attached to them in a more formal situation.

23

It is again a question of fitness-for-purpose. If the teacher simply wants imme-diate feedback on his work, he is likely to get the best results from an informal discussion with the group, and shortcomings in technique (badly phrased ques-tions, for example) can be corrected as he goes along. However, if he has to measure the standard of work attained, say, for an end-of-term report, then this method would almost certainly be too casual and inaccurate.

An understanding of the principles of test construction, therefore, is essential, not just so that the teacher can design his own tests but because this under-standing enables him to decide when a test needs to be rigorously constructed, when informal methods are appropriate and what interpretation should be placed on the marks obtained from these different sources.

Assessment and the curriculum

We have stressed the importance of assessment in teaching; some people also find it an interesting area of study. But it is not of overriding importance and it would be unwise to get so carried away by enthusiasm for testing that no teaching (or learning) ever got done.

Equally, we have pointed out that it would be foolish to take the attitude that, because a good test exists, one should teach to it so that it can be used. Tests, examinations and assessment need to be considered in relation to the whole context of the teaching programme.

Figure 2 illustrates the relationship between assessment and the teaching programme by showing a model of curriculum design.

Starting with AIMS, the teacher planning his syllabus would ask himself 'Why am I teaching this course? What is it going to do for the pupils?'

Then moving on to the more detailed objectives, he would try to establish exactly what the children should know at the end of the course and what they should be able to do then that they could not do before it started. And having decided this, he would choose the most effective method of achieving these aims and objectives; perhaps a team-teaching approach would be most appropriate, or discovery methods, or he might want to introduce group work in mixed-ability classes.

All through this preliminary planning stage, a more or less continuous process of evaluation will be going on: the teacher must consider whether the aims and objectives are in accord with the general philosophy of the school, whether the chosen method is practicable in view of the staff available, whether there is ade-quate accommodation and equipment, and so on.

Having worked out solutions to these problems, the teacher can design the course, planning the sequence of learning experiences to be offered to the pupils, the books to be used, films, visits, practical sessions, etc. With these should also

24

be planned the assessment procedures that will be needed and the appropriate technique chosen to match the particular teaching situation. For example, does the school require termly reports or form orders? How much information is required? Are there end-of-term exams? Will the pupils be doing a lot of work on their own? If so, how can a check be kept on their progress? Does the course lead to an external examination? If so, will there be mock examinations, and when? What sort of records are to be kept, and by whom?

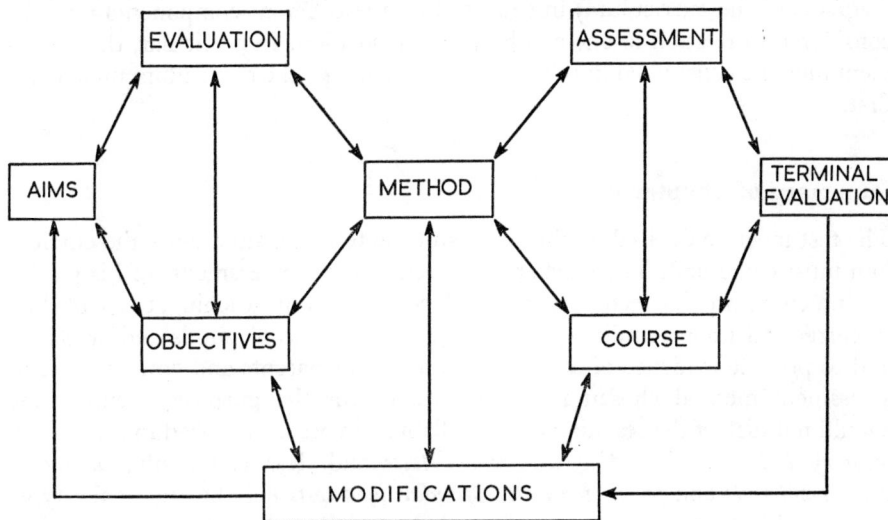

Fig. 2 Relationship between assessment and the curriculum

At the end of this stage of the planning exercise (and when the whole course has been worked through in practice) there must be a terminal evaluation, when the whole scheme is looked at. As a result of this scrutiny, there will almost certainly be modifications to be made to some or all of the preceding elements, so the process becomes one of continuous revision and improvement.

Perhaps the process described above is an idealized one and in practice a teacher might well start the procedure at a point on the diagram other than the left-hand side. The head of economics in a sixth-form college, for example, decided that he wanted to change to a team-teaching method because (*a*) it was a waste of resources to have four different teachers explaining the same basic principles to four different groups at the same time and (*b*) developments in the subject are so rapid that the department, as a whole, could keep abreast of current thinking better if individual members of staff could concentrate on particular aspects. The saving in staff time allowed the school to employ part-time secretarial help, thus permitting the development of many more teaching aids (film strips, tables of data, copies of newspaper articles, etc.) and the establishment of a storage and retrieval system for the rapidly growing stock of resource material. The new method required a redesigning of the course (and associated assessment procedures to enable an evaluation of its effectiveness to be made) and inevitably also caused reconsideration of aims and objectives.

The main point, therefore, is not that there must be a linear sequence of steps to be taken in curriculum design (though this makes for convenience in drawing diagrams of the curriculum) but rather that the different components must be considered in relation to one another, not in isolation. In particular, the assessment must be considered in relation to the teaching – the curriculum must come first.

Summary of Chapter I

The test must be devised or chosen to suit the teaching situation – the curriculum must come first. The teacher may need to make assessments of his pupils' attainment to provide feedback on the effectiveness of his teaching, to enable him to correct misunderstandings, to monitor the progress of pupils and/or classes and to provide evidence of school attainments for parents and employers. The assessment method chosen must be suitable for the purpose intended and should not distort the teaching or the syllabus. Types of test used in schools are *mastery tests, discriminating attainment tests* and, less commonly, *diagnostic attainment tests* and *predictive tests. Standardized tests* may be any of the types mentioned but have been prepared so that results can be related to a standard or average result.

Questions on Chapter I

(Outline answers are given in Appendix A.)

1 A geography teacher wants to include a large amount of field work in the fourth and fifth years. Some parents, however, express concern that this may prejudice the children's chances when they come to take external examinations. What steps could the geography teacher take to find out whether or not this is likely to be the case?

2 Because of the difficulty of organizing a large-scale practical test, a teacher of handicraft bases end-of-term marks on the results of a written examination. What information would be needed before the value of these assessments could be estimated?

3 The history panel of an examining board decides to include a project as well as an essay paper and an objective test in its examination. The panel states that, in the project, candidates should show their ability to:

i select, organize and interpret historical material from a variety of sources;
ii present historical arguments and draw conclusions from the evidence, analyse a historical character or situation and show an empathetic understanding of the past;
iii conduct an inquiry over a period of time on a topic of historical interest and present the results in readable form.

a Would these aims also be appropriate for the examination as a whole?
b Would a project, say, on Education before 1914, and consisting of tape-recorded interviews with old people be acceptable for this examination?

Assignments

1 Consider the four main types of test in relation to your own subject, and look for cases in which each might be used. Where would a standardized test be appropriate or useful?
2 What is the purpose of the assessments carried out in your own school? What use is made of the information (a) within your own class, (b) within the department, (c) within the school as a whole? What function is served by the public examination, if one is taken?
3 Choose a particular unit of your own teaching programme; state the objectives of this unit and show how this part of the course attempts to achieve these objectives. Suggest appropriate assessment procedures to be used:

a to enable you to evaluate the effectiveness of your teaching,
b to provide information for the end-of-term report.

Suggestions for further reading

Several topics have been touched on in the course of this chapter which are outside the scope of this book. Readers who wish to investigate further will find some suggestions below. All of these books are reasonably straightforward; they all contain lists of references which can lead on to further study.

On the curriculum
HOOPER, R. (ed.) *The Curriculum: Context, Design and Development.* Oliver & Boyd, 1971.
NICHOLLS, A. and H. *Developing a Curriculum: a Practical Guide.* Allen & Unwin, 1972.

RICHMOND, W. KENNETH. *The School Curriculum*. Methuen, Education Paperbacks, 1971.

On psychological testing
BUTCHER, H. J. *Human Intelligence: Its Nature and Assessment*. Methuen, University Paperbacks, 1970.
(An introduction to this subject.)

On standardized tests
JACKSON, S. *A Teacher's Guide to Tests and Testing*. Longmans Green, 1968.
SCHOFIELD, H. *Assessment and Testing: an Introduction*. Unwin Educational, 1972.
(Deals with essay tests, subjective and objective marking as well as with intelligence tests, prognostic and diagnostic tests, aptitude tests, psychomotor tests, etc.)

Catalogues of currently available standardized tests are obtainable from Ginn and Company Ltd (Test Services), Elsinore House, Buckingham Street, Aylesbury, Bucks., and from NFER Publishing Company Ltd, 2 Jennings Buildings, Thames Avenue, Windsor, Bucks.

Information and advice on the use of standardized tests can be obtained from the Principal Research Officer, Guidance and Assessment Service, the National Foundation for Educational Research in England and Wales, The Mere, Upton Park, Slough, Berks.

II. Designing a classroom test

In this chapter, we shall consider the construction of a discriminating attainment test – a pencil-and-paper test for use in the classroom. We shall concentrate mainly on the short-answer type of test because, although the principles involved are applicable to a much wider range of test situations, we hope that they can be more easily appreciated in a limited context first. For this reason, we would recommend that even those readers whose main interest may be in the assessment of practical work or in oral examining, for example, should study this chapter, in any case as far as p. 38.

We have talked in general terms about the need to ensure fitness-for-purpose; we shall now look at two vitally important aspects of this requirement: the test must be valid and it must be reliable.

Validity

Basically, validity means making sure that the test does what it is meant to do.

There are several different sorts of validity; the first we shall consider is *face validity*. This means that the test should look as if it is testing what it is intended to test. In some forms of psychological testing, face validity is made deliberately low in order to prevent those being tested giving misleading answers; because these tests may be investigating very intimate and sensitive aspects of personality, it is sometimes necessary to engage in a form of deceit and to pretend that the test is aimed at something quite different. With a school attainment test, it is not necessary to go to such lengths and good face validity is important. If a teacher judges, from his experience, that a test looks right for the particular purpose intended, then there is a reasonable chance that he is on the right lines. It seems fairer, also, that the pupils should be clear about what is being tested so that they can direct their energies accordingly.

Face validity, however, is only a starting-point and it is not enough, on its own, to feel that the test looks right. Another form of validity is *criterion-related validity* – the relationship between scores on the test and some other criterion such as teachers' estimates or results on an external examination. Criterion-related validity can be *concurrent* (test results compared with another measure of the same abilities at the same time) or *predictive* (test results compared later with another criterion such as success in a particular job or at university). Obviously, estimates of criterion-related validity depend crucially on what the criterion is

29

and it must be remembered that there may be variability in the criterion itself, in addition to that in the test which is being compared with it. Criterion-related validity can be important to the teacher if he needs to use the test as a 'filter' – to decide entries for a public examination, for example – though it can be difficult to work out. Some consideration of the method of comparing results from different sources is given in Chapter V.

Undoubtedly the most important aspect of validity for the teacher is *content validity* – the extent to which the test adequately covers the syllabus area to be tested.

Content validity

To have good content validity a test must reflect both the content and the balance of the teaching which led up to it.

First, the length of the test must be considered: a very short test could probably not cover a year's work. Equally, to cover a year's work completely, a very long test might be needed. Therefore, unless a lot of tests are given at frequent intervals, the syllabus must be sampled, that is to say, not everything is tested, but a representative selection of the most important topics is made.

The selection of topics is critically important. It is not just a matter of including a number of questions on each topic. The selection must be made, and the test questions prepared, in such a way that they also reflect the way in which the topics were treated during the course. It is necessary, therefore, to be quite clear as to the objectives of the teaching, to identify the skills, knowledge and understanding that are to be developed during this part of the syllabus so that the appropriate technique can be chosen to test them.

It should be possible to achieve high content validity with a teacher-made test; if care and thought have gone into the analysis of teaching objectives and course content (thus providing a framework for the design of the test) then it should be possible to prepare the test material so as to match this analysis very closely.

A standardized test can also be valid for a particular school, if, after a similar analysis, it can be shown to match the teaching aims (as in the example of the remedial English class, p. 15).

An invalid test, on the other hand, is useless. It will not give the information which is required and it will be utterly unfair to the children who may have worked hard preparing for it only to find that their efforts have been wasted because something quite unexpected is being measured.

It is worth while taking a lot of trouble over validity. One way of ensuring good content validity is to prepare a *test blueprint* or *specification grid*. This simply means writing down those aspects of the course which are to be tested, in the form of a table, as shown in Table 1. In this example, a physics teacher

30

has completed a series of lessons on magnetism and electricity with a third-year group. He wishes to test recall of facts, understanding and knowledge of certain laws and principles as applicable to three areas: the magnetic effect of a current, the effect of force on a conductor and electromagnetic induction. This gives two sides of the grid. The teacher then decides on the number of questions

Table 1 Test specification for a third-year physics group

Ability to be tested	Magnetic effect of a current	Effect of force on a conductor	Electromagnetic induction	Number of questions
Factual recall	4	3	3	10
Understanding	5	6	4	15
Knowledge of laws and principles	1	2	2	5
Total marks	10	11	9	30

to be set in each section, depending on its importance and the stress he laid on it in his teaching. He would also decide on the weighting to be attached to each question: for example, he might feel that, although there may be only 5 questions to be set on laws and principles, these are so important that they are worth more marks than the questions involving recall of facts and so he could weight these questions twice or three times as heavily.

Table 2 Specification for a first-year French vocabulary test

Knowledge tested	la famille	la maison	la ville	Number of questions
Nouns	4	6	4	14
Adjectives	2	2	—	4
Verbs	1	1	3	5
Adverbs, prepositions, etc.	1	2	4	7
Total marks	8	11	11	30

Depending on the level of the test, it may not be necessary to specify separate skills in the way shown above. The next example (Table 2) shows a specification for a French vocabulary test for a first-year class where the teacher is concerned with testing just one area: knowledge of the meaning of words which have been introduced in the early stages of the course.

It must be stressed that drawing up a specification in this form does not necessarily imply that the test itself should involve the use of grammatical terms. At this stage, they are no more than a guide for the teacher; depending on the teaching method adopted, he might test the meaning by using pictures, by asking for English equivalents, by questions in French or by sentence completion items, or by a combination of several of these methods.

The specification grid is quite often used in public examinations to allow the subject panel to instruct the examiners as to what sort of examination or test to set. In the school test situation, however, this particular function is not likely to be important and it can be equally satisfactory if a retrospective specification is drawn up. By this, we mean that the teacher writes his test questions in the normal way and then analyses them along similar lines to those shown in Table 2, to see if there are any omissions or if any unconscious bias has crept in, perhaps giving undue stress to one aspect of the course.

It is important that the test is given some sort of check, even if it is a very informal one (it is not always necessary to write it all out, for example) and, if time permits, it is best to do it both before and after the test has been set.

Certain points must be made clear about these examples. First, content validity is very much a matter of individual judgement and this judgement must be exercised in relation to what each individual teacher is trying to do. Therefore, the particular examples given are in no sense models or ideal blueprints to be copied blindly; another teacher might have quite a different approach and would devise a completely different test specification – for example, another physics teacher might wish to include some calculations or he might have done some work on Ohm's law which should be included. Similarly, at a later stage in the French course, the teacher would certainly want to test usage and forms of words, not just their meaning.

Secondly, because we are restricting ourselves to pencil-and-paper tests, there is no reference to orals, practical work, etc. A full specification of assessment procedures for the whole course would undoubtedly have to cover more abilities and skills than are illustrated in our examples. Further, there may well be aspects even of those abilities which are included which must be additionally tested in some other way, by essays, by investigational work, and so on.

Thirdly, it must be remembered that, even following the same specification, there is potentially an almost infinite number of tests that could be set; practical considerations restrict the teacher to perhaps 30 questions or so and when he sets the test he writes a particular group of 30. He could choose to write 30 quite different but equally valid questions, thus producing a new test on the same topics. But the particular set of questions he does decide to use will have a different effect on individual pupils; someone may strike lucky by getting all the 'right' questions while another unfortunate gets asked about all the topics where

32

he is a bit shaky. This third point is really more a question of reliability which will be dealt with further in the following section.

The importance of validity and, in the context of school attainment tests, of content validity must be stressed again. It is certainly not an easy task to ensure that a test is valid; the specification of teaching objectives alone is often a difficult operation. Nevertheless, it is a problem which must be tackled. It takes time and effort to set, work through and mark any test, valid or not. But if the test is invalid, this is time and effort wasted, by both teacher and pupils. It is essential that this energy is directed towards a worth-while goal and, if a test has to be set, then it must be a good one.

Reliability

For our purposes, we can define reliability as consistency, that is, how far the same test (or a similar one) would give the same results if it could be done again by the same children under the same conditions.

The definition is, of course, a theoretical one because the same conditions can never be achieved with the same children – the mere fact that they have done the test once makes things different on the second run; even if the test itself is not identical on the second occasion, the children will have learned (or forgotten) some things in the interval between the two.

So we can never expect to get a perfectly reliable test. Even in physical measurements, scientists know that perfect accuracy and consistency cannot be achieved; it is not surprising that the measurement of mental abilities is subject to even greater variability.

It is important, however, to do whatever can be done to reduce this variability and it is possible to identify three main sources:

i   *Variation in the performance of the person taking the test*
     All kinds of extraneous influences may affect a child's performance on the day of the test – physical health, domestic problems, a quarrel in the playground, excitement about an approaching birthday party, the strain of taking the test itself, and so on. There is little that the teacher can do about these factors, except to take any known external influences into account when interpreting the results and to investigate further if any sudden, inexplicable changes are observed in a child's attainment.

ii   *Variations in the test*
     As we pointed out previously, the test that is actually given is only one of a large number of possible tests which could be set on the same topics. The test can only measure a small sample of the child's ability in the subject and a different sample might give a different result.

33

iii   *Variation in the marking*

If the marking is other than completely objective (i.e. each answer can be marked unequivocally right or wrong), then the marker's judgement can vary for much the same sort of reasons as the child's performance can vary. This problem is at its most severe in marking essays (particularly in external examinations when perhaps 60 examiners are each marking 400–500 scripts) but it exists also in marking short-answer tests. For example, interruptions during the course of marking may cause different standards to be applied after the break, standards of judgement may alter after marking a series of very good (or very bad) test papers, or the teacher may subconsciously be influenced by his knowledge of a particular pupil.

The effects of the first two sources of variation can be lessened by giving a series of several tests at intervals, though since (we hope) the children will be making continued progress, the tests must change to match this and the results cannot be compared directly. Nevertheless, it is reasonable to suppose that things will even themselves out over a period of time. The third type of variation can be reduced by similar methods (i.e. by using several markers) but this is not likely to be practicable. Alternatively, care must be given to the marking method, both in the design of the test and when actually marking the papers to ensure consistency (see pp. 36–42).

It will be apparent from this discussion that there are quite severe limitations on the accuracy of any tests that can be devised. This is not to say that one need not bother about reliability. Even though the best test we can make will be less than perfect, it is easily possible to make one which is very much worse. The implication, rather, is that when we obtain marks from a test, we should view them with a degree of humility and scepticism, recognizing the fallibility of the techniques at our disposal.

Interaction between validity and reliability

The two are, as we have seen, closely linked together but validity is the first consideration: a test which is not valid is useless and it does not matter whether it is reliable or not.

On the other hand, a test which is totally unreliable *could not be valid* because its results would depend on chance, not on attainment in the subject. Reliability is a necessary condition of validity, but not a sufficient one; that is to say, a test can be reliable without being valid but, to be valid, a test *must* be reliable *and also* satisfy the other requirements outlined in the section on validity, pp. 29–33.

This is a difficult area because there are no absolutes: it is unlikely that any school attainment test, no matter how badly set, would be totally invalid or wholly unreliable. But if we try to improve one aspect, we may find that this causes a reduction of the other and it calls for skilled professional judgement to decide the extent to which this occurs in a particular case and whether it is acceptable.

Perhaps we can illustrate the relationship between validity and reliability by an analogy with a fielder in cricket trying to throw the ball so as to hit the stumps. If he hits them every time, we could say his throw was both valid (the right target) and reliable (that is, consistent). His throw might be valid (aimed at the stumps) but sometimes not very reliable (when it misses them). However, if the throw arrived in the general area of the stumps, it could be gathered by the wicket-keeper and might still be useful – much more so, in fact, than if we tried to get perfect reliability and found that the fielder could guarantee to hit a target every time only if it was no more than a couple of yards away from where he was standing.

If, of course, his throwing was completely unreliable, so that he was just as likely to hit anything in sight – other fielders, a tree on the boundary, an old gentleman asleep by the pavilion – then the question of what he thought he was trying to hit would be quite irrelevant. Or, if he was ignorant of the rules of cricket and always threw at the wrong target, it would, equally, be immaterial whether his throw was reliable or not.

These are extreme and rather unlikely cases and most people can throw more or less in the right direction, but it is the direction, the target, which is important; having established that, one can then try to improve the accuracy of the throwing. So it is with testing: the aim of the test must be established and one must then use the most reliable methods consistent with that aim. Reliability on its own is pointless; validity without reliability is not possible, because one is then depending on chance.

Returning to the school attainment test, then, there are ways in which reliability and certain types of validity* can be calculated. Some elementary techniques are given in Chapter V but readers who wish to follow-up further are advised to study any of the standard textbooks on educational measurement and statistics which are listed in the references at the end of this chapter.

However, it is fair to give a warning that some of the calculations in these texts are quite involved; although many of the basic operations can be managed, particularly if the school has one of the small electronic calculators which are now available, there is a limit to their usefulness with the comparatively small numbers the teacher is concerned with. Indeed, in some cases, the use of sophisticated analyses with small numbers may even give misleading results because experimental error, caused by the inevitable inaccuracy of our test methods, is

* Criterion-related validity in particular, but also construct validity and factorial validity, which are too complex to be considered here.

exaggerated when only a small number of results is analysed. What is likely to be of more practical utility in the school situation is that the teacher should be aware of the factors affecting the validity and reliability of the tests he is making and take steps to improve them.

Factors affecting reliability and validity

i   *Length of test*
Syllabus coverage has been mentioned already. Other things being equal, a short test will be less valid and less reliable than a long one (but merely lengthening an invalid or unreliable test is no guarantee of improving it).

ii   *Choice of test technique*
Essay questions tend to be less reliable than short-answer questions. Structured or 'guided' essays (i.e. where the question is subdivided into several parts or where instructions are given to deal with certain aspects of the subject) are usually more reliable than a completely open subject, where just a title or 'Discuss . . . ' is given; essays where a factual content is required (e.g. in history) are likely to be more reliably marked than, say, creative writing in English composition. Short-answer tests, sentence completion items or diagram or map labelling tend to be fairly reliable (though their validity must be carefully considered) because a large number can be set in a short time (see above), because the children are in little doubt about how to deal with them (whereas the decision on how to treat an open essay subject may be very difficult) and because they can be marked consistently and accurately. A well-prepared objective test* can also be highly reliable but the preparation of it is not easy and a badly constructed one can be, in many ways, the worst of all.

Nevertheless, improved reliability is not a reason for choosing an invalid test technique; for example, to test creative writing in English, even a well-constructed objective test would be quite inappropriate.

iii   *Technique of writing questions*
Vaguely worded questions, ambiguous questions, trick questions or questions using obscure vocabulary or complicated syntax adversely affect validity and reliability; the score on the test will depend in part on attainment in the subject concerned and in part on how quick the child is at spotting the hidden catch, how lucky in guessing the 'right' meaning of the ambiguity or how sophisticated his grasp of English.

* The most familiar form of objective test is the multiple-choice, where pupils have to mark the correct answer out of several possible answers printed on the test paper.

iv *Method of administration*

Adequate time should be allowed for most of the group to finish the test (excluding any unusually slow children) otherwise wild guessing will be encouraged, a premium put on the slick and facile answer and the test will become one of speed, not of attainment. Unclear instructions can adversely affect both validity and reliability; if the children are in doubt about what they have to do, some may become confused, some will answer one way and some another and the results of the test will be of little value. The physical conditions under which the test is taken are also important. Pupils must have room to write, adequate lighting, pen, pencil, blotting paper and rubber as needed; there must also be some means of ensuring that they are working independently.

v *Method of marking*

As far as possible, the marking should be objective, that is to say, each pupil should get the same mark, no matter when or by whom his test paper is marked.

Obviously, where essay-type questions are concerned this is very difficult. The two concepts of reliability and validity are again involved; one would have a very reliable measure if one simply counted, say, the number of words in the essays but it would not be valid. Ways in which the reliability of essay marking can be improved will be suggested in Chapter III. For the time being, it is important to remember that marking which depends on the exercise of judgement is subject to all the normal variations of human fallibility and cannot be relied on to be absolutely accurate or consistent.

With short-answer tests it should be possible to achieve more reliable standards of marking though the degree of judgement which has to be exercised obviously tends to vary with the length of the answer. Where only a single word is required and the choice of words is very restricted, it should be possible to mark the test objectively (though a decision has to be made on the importance or otherwise of correct spelling, etc.). If a sentence, or part of a sentence, is required as an answer, there can be differences of opinion about how correct the answer is or whether it is correctly expressed or what is meant by a badly worded response, etc. and the problem of ensuring reliable marking increases.*

The objective test (as its name implies) should be capable of being marked completely objectively, i.e. it could be marked by someone without any

---

* If several sentences or a short paragraph are needed to answer, the test becomes more like an essay test and considerations of essay marking should apply.

specialist knowledge, or even by a machine, because all the allowable answers are printed on the test paper and each one is either right or wrong.

It should be stressed, however, that although it is very easy to mark objective and short-answer questions quickly, it is also surprisingly easy to make careless errors; the mechanical and repetitive nature of the marking tends to lull one into a kind of trance and one is often unpleasantly surprised later to discover the number of lapses that have occurred. It is always wise to check the accuracy of the marking (the pupils will be glad to make a very rigorous check if the papers are returned to them) before the final record of results is made.

How to make a better test – checklist

In this section, we give a checklist of points to watch out for when actually preparing a test. Many of the points made will be familiar to experienced teachers but we hope, nevertheless, that the list will be of use as a reminder.

i   *Allow plenty of time for preparation.*
Making a test should not be rushed. We recognize that pressures on teachers are often so great that the ideal cannot always be achieved but we would strongly recommend, particularly to newcomers to the profession, that as much time as possible should be left for preparation of the test.

ii   *Prepare a test blueprint or specification grid.*
This is a way of ensuring content validity (see pp. 30–3). The skills, abilities or knowledge which should have been acquired or developed during the period of the course which is to be tested must be clearly established. These are set out in the form of a table and questions are set in each category to reflect the balance of the teaching.

Alternatively, an analysis of the test may be made after the questions have been written, to check that syllabus coverage is adequate. Ideally, both procedures should be carried out.

iii *Prepare more test material than you think you will need.*
At a later stage, you may reject some questions and it is easier just to eliminate them rather than having to think up new ones to fill the gaps.

iv   *Avoid, if possible, allowing a choice of questions.*
A choice of questions complicates everything. First, the children have to make the choice and it is often only too apparent that some choose the wrong

ones and fail to do themselves justice; and, second, for a choice to be valid the questions should either all be of equal difficulty (which is almost impossible to ensure) or the hard ones should carry more marks (and it is equally difficult to decide beforehand how much harder one is than another).

When the children have chosen different questions, they are in effect doing different tests* and it is one of the most difficult tasks of all to compare the performance of one child on one test with another on a different one. There may be reasons why a choice has to be allowed, for example, in an external examination to give schools some flexibility in choice of syllabus areas. The examining board's examiners, however, have to expend considerable care to make sure that the questions are truly comparable; with school tests, it is best to avoid these problems wherever possible by making all questions compulsory.

v   *Set the test at a reasonable level of difficulty for the pupils.*
Sometimes people get the idea that they are setting laudably high standards by giving a very hard test. All that happens in fact is that all the children get low marks and the purpose of a discriminating test – to separate different levels of ability – is defeated because they all bunch together at the bottom.

Of course, in a streamed school, if the same test is given to all streams, you might well find that not many children in the lowest stream get very high marks, which is to be expected. In this case, the test should be at a reasonable level for all streams, that is to say, even the weakest pupils should find something that they can do. Quite apart from the depressing effect, if many children get zero on a test it tells you nothing about their abilities relative to one another. (Equally, if a lot get top marks, you learn nothing about the relative abilities of this group either.)

vi   *Avoid setting questions on trivial or obscure points.*
It is also a mistake to think that a test is made harder by including questions on minuscule details or on marginally relevant points which have been relegated to a footnote in the text. It is more likely to reduce validity because even the best pupils may have overlooked such information or disregarded it as unimportant.

* If you have to choose 8 questions out of 10, there is a possibility of 45 different tests, choosing 7 out of 10 allows 120 different tests, 6 out of 10, 210, and so on. *Two* papers, each allowing a choice of 5 questions out of 10, give 63 504 possible combinations.

For example, in a test on this checklist we could set a question asking how many different tests there are if you have to choose 6 questions out of 10 (see footnote on p. 39). But the main point was that a choice of questions causes problems in marking and that the more the choice, the greater the problems – the precise number is only an illustration and remembering it (or not) is unlikely to affect anyone's understanding of the text.

Questions to which the answers are debatable should be avoided in a short-answer test. Even if it is considered that, at this particular stage in the course, the pupils are not yet aware of different opinions, there is always the risk that some child may have access to more information than the others and be put off by the complications in answering what was intended to be a perfectly straightforward question.

vii *Do not set trick questions.*
Question **3b** at the end of Chapter I is an example of a trick question. In this kind of question the pupil has to spot perhaps a particular word or number in a sentence which appears to be asking about something quite different. Those pupils who do spot the trick may feel that they have been very clever (and one sometimes gets the impression that the examiner feels the same at having set it) but whatever is being tested, it is not attainment in the subject.

viii *Phrase the questions clearly and unambiguously.*
Convoluted syntax and unnecessarily long words* should be avoided – the aim is not to show the erudition of the test setter but to test attainment in a subject. Do not use an obscure word where a simple one (or several simple ones) will do – the test can too easily turn into one of linguistic comprehension. In particular, questions with double negatives or 'not . . . unless' and 'not . . . except' tend to confuse.

ix *Make sure that the questions are independent.*
If, for example, question 2 can only be answered if question 1 has been answered correctly, then the child who does not know the answer to question 1 is doubly penalized – and he might have got question 2 right if he had the chance.

x *Make sure that the answer to one question is not given as part of another.*
This can happen by oversight, especially if a fairly long test is being prepared. Be careful, too, that unconscious clues are not given in the wording

---

* Long words which form part of the technical vocabulary of the subject, and which the children must know in order to progress, are fair enough, however.

of the questions or by the size of the space allowed for answering – unless you deliberately want to cue the answers in this way.

xi *Give clear instructions how to answer.*
Even if it is felt that the class knows what to do, put instructions on how to answer at the top of the test paper – there will always be one or two children who forget. It is also wise to tell them what to do at the beginning of the session, particularly routine points such as writing names on answer sheets; get the group to do this before starting the test, because anonymous scripts can be a great nuisance later.

Instructions should be simple and complete; they should include things such as whether to answer on the test paper, on a special answer sheet or on plain paper, whether a full sentence or only a word or two is needed, whether incorrect spelling loses marks, whether working for mathematical problems is required, the marks allotted to the questions and the time allowed for answering.

If the test is composed of questions that have to be answered in different ways, group the different types together into sections and put the appropriate instructions at the beginning of each section.

xii *Avoid questions which can be answered 'yes' or 'no'.*
Even if you explain that a sentence is required as an answer, a question such as 'Did the 1944 Education Act represent a major advance in secondary education in this country?' invites the answer 'Yes, it did' or 'No, it didn't'. The question should be specific: 'Give one (or two etc.) reason(s) why . . .'

xiii *Plan the layout of the test carefully.*
Attention should be given to the layout of the test paper so that it is easy to read; if at all possible, the test paper should be typed and duplicated so that each pupil has a copy. It is worth while also thinking about how it is to be answered: adequate space must be allowed for the answers to be written in. If the test is to be reused, it will be more economical if answers are written on a separate sheet, in which case it is probably easier for the children if a special answer sheet is prepared, in which the spaces for the answers are matched to the spacing of questions on the test paper and numbered in the same way.

Marking the test will be simplified if arrangements can be made at this stage for all the answers to be written at the same place on the page – down the right-hand side, for example – and space should be left for the mark to go beside each answer.

xiv *Prepare model answers and mark scheme.*
Having written the questions, the answers expected should be written down; try to think of all the possible correct answers and some of the likely wrong ones as well. This should help to gauge the difficulty of the test. Decide how the test is to be marked and what each question is worth (though it frequently happens that the mark scheme has to be modified when the actual answers come in).

If the layout of the test permits, it will speed up the marking if a marking template is prepared. At its simplest, this need mean no more than a copy of the test paper with the correct answers written in; this is laid partly over the sheet to be marked so that the two answers can be compared. Slightly more elaborate is the preparation of a sheet of card with holes cut in it to correspond to the spaces on the test paper where the pupils' answers are to be written and the correct answers are written on the card beside each aperture. It makes for more accurate adding up of scores if all the ticks or crosses appear at the same side of the answer sheet, even if the actual answers do not.

xv *After preparing the test, leave it on one side for a week or so and re-read it.*
It is often surprising what shortcomings can be seen after a period of time: ambiguities, bad wording, unclear instructions, etc.

xvi *Get a colleague to read through the material.*
A second opinion is extremely valuable and someone else may spot weaknesses that the writer of the test has missed.

xvii *After giving the test, study the results carefully.*
We shall deal with some ways of doing this in Chapter VI. Briefly, it means that often more information can be obtained from a test than just the total mark and also that an analysis of the test will usually show ways in which it can be improved.

Amount of work in test preparation

All this involves a lot of work. It is true that educational testing is not easy and that it must be done carefully if it is to be done at all. However, with experience, many of the points above become matters of routine and the whole operation can be speeded up considerably without cutting any corners. Sensible planning beforehand can help to avoid a sudden rush at one particular time, though it is recognized that the vagaries of school life, with speech days, sports days, choir practices, rehearsals for the school play, etc., can upset any programme and last-minute adjustments may have to be made. Nevertheless, we think that assessment is an important part of teaching and adequate time must be allotted for doing it properly. The conclusion must be that if it takes a long time to make a test, then testing should be done on fewer occasions and done better; the opposite procedure (to test badly and often) is a waste of everyone's time.

Perhaps some teachers test too often; others may not do enough. It is necessary to strike a reasonable balance, but the preparation of the test, when it is decided that one is necessary, must not be skimped.

Types of classroom test

The following are examples of the main types of classroom tests. The examples are taken from various subjects as illustrations only; the methods will, of course, be appropriate to other subjects also.

i   *Direct questions*
    What is the name given to an alloy of copper and zinc?
    Expected answer: Brass

    Who was in command of the Prussian army at the battle of Waterloo?
    Expected answer: Blücher

    Que faites-vous le matin à huit heures?
    Expected answer: Je me lève

The first two examples are fairly straightforward and the answers can probably be marked unequivocally right or wrong. The third, however, illustrates the difficulties that can arise. Perhaps the teacher has been working on reflexive verbs and most of the class will give the expected answer. But some may answer 'Je dors' or 'Je mange le petit déjeuner' or 'J'attends l'autobus au coin de la rue'. Are these acceptable? Is a child who attempts a very elaborate answer and makes some mistakes as good as one who plays safe with the bare minimum?

ii *Sentence completion*
    Le matin, à huit heures, je me . . . . . .
    Expected answers: lève, lave, réveille

This restricts the answer to the reflexive verb though, in this case, the child who answers 'je m'habille' is being invited to make a mistake by omitting to delete the vowel in 'me'.

> Chalk is an example of a . . . . . . rock.
> Expected answer: sedimentary

But one might answer 'permeable', 'soft' or even 'white'. To test understanding of the term 'sedimentary', it would be better to turn the question round:

> One type of sedimentary rock is . . . . . .
> Acceptable answers: limestone, chalk, etc.

It may be acceptable to omit more than one word in a sentence completion question, though care must be taken that too much of the sentence is not left out or it may become incomprehensible.

iii *True/false questions*
Transpiration means the passage of moisture from the leaves to the root of a plant: True/False
Expected answer: False

It is possible with this type for pupils to get the right answer for the wrong reasons, e.g. in the example above, False might be marked even though the pupil had confused transpiration with aspiration. A check on this is to ask for the reason ('False – because transpiration is the loss of moisture by evaporation from the leaves') though this complicates the marking.

It is not always easy to find statements which are unarguably right or wrong; it is much easier if the statement is related to specific information given on the test paper, such as a comprehension passage, a table of figures, a map or diagram, etc. The questions can then be set in the form 'According to the passage . . .' or 'The diagram shows that . . .', rather than in terms of universal truth.

Guessing can be a factor with True/False questions; obviously there is a 50/50 chance of getting it right. Asking for the reason for the False answer is one way of reducing this; another is to introduce a third category: Impossible to say, which can be done when the questions are on information given on the paper and in some cases the information is deliberately insufficient to decide whether the statement is true or not. It is probably advisable to have roughly equal numbers of true and false items; if Impossible to say is included, it is not necessary to have very many genuine examples of this category, probably not more than a quarter of the total.

There is a tendency to make true statements longer than false ones because

44

one includes more qualifications to make sure that the true statement *is* true. The test should be checked through to see that unconscious clues of this kind are not given.

iv *Diagram or map labelling*

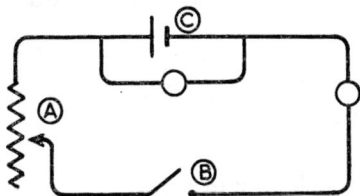

What is the meaning of the symbol shown on the diagram at: A . . . . . .
B . . . . . .
C . . . . . .?

Expected answers: Variable resistance
Switch
Battery

Pupils can be asked to write the answers directly on the diagram though there may be problems of space and it is usually more convenient to have the answers written separately. It should also be remembered that some children have a habit of writing things on diagrams in such a way that the word falls equidistant between two of the points, thus serving for either.

Variations of this technique are to list the names required and to ask the children either to associate them with the given code letters or to write the word (or a code letter) at the correct place on the diagram or map.

The difficulty of this type of test can be increased if more words are listed than there are spaces to be labelled (or the reverse) so that more discrimination has to be exercised; obviously if you are given five words and five spaces, the last word is self-selecting to fill the last space.

v *Diagram or map drawing, sketches*
If the children are asked to make diagrams, maps or sketches either to illustrate answers or as a separate question, it is important to make quite certain of the reason why they should do this and how the question is to be marked. For example, is the artistic appeal of the diagram important or is it irrelevant to the particular subject concerned? Is the ability to draw a map from memory vital or would the same purpose be achieved by providing an outline? It seems only fair, too, if the children know the criteria which are to be applied.

Some authorities classify true/false and diagram labelling as objective tests and, certainly, they can be marked objectively. Most people, though, associate the term with multiple-choice items (and similar types of question) such as:

A paint suitable for decorating exterior woodwork is: (A) distemper
(B) enamel
(C) creosote
(D) cellulose.

Expected answer: (B)

Multiple-choice items look easy to set and some people develop a knack for writing them. However, it is as easy to write bad items as good ones and it is often impossible to tell which are good or which are bad until the test has been tried out. It is generally agreed, therefore, that an objective test needs to be pre-tested – tried out first with a group of pupils similar to those who will be taking the final test – and the results analysed so that unsatisfactory items can be eliminated.* It is unlikely that in many schools there will be the facilities or the time for doing this, so we would not recommend that teachers attempt to devise objective tests unless special expertise and resources are available. It may seem a tempting alternative to use one of the published books of objective tests in various subjects which are now available, but we would recommend that they are approached with caution. In some cases, their antecedents are doubtful; they may be of some use for revision or to allow the children to become used to the technique (which does not usually take long), but they should not be used as part of a school test programme unless full information is given on the design of the test, the sample of pupils with whom the tests were tried out and the results obtained, so that reliability and validity can be assessed.

We would repeat the warning that a bad objective test is very bad indeed, and the problems of making a good one are worth a book on their own; for this reason we suggest that teachers who are interested in this aspect should refer to some of the texts recommended at the end of the chapter.

Summary of Chapter II

In designing a classroom test, careful attention must be given to the validity of the test and its reliability. The technique chosen should be appropriate to the purpose of the assessment and adequate time should be allowed for preparation of the test. Short-answer questions, sentence completion, true/false items and

* The example given has *not* been pre-tested.

diagram labelling are commonly used techniques which can be fairly reliable, provided that they are valid for the particular assessment which the teacher wishes to make.

Questions on Chapter II

(Outline answers are given in Appendix A.)

1 On a 20-item test, taken by a whole year-group, the marks achieved by a middle-stream class of 22 children were as follows:

14, 12, 11, 11, 9, 8, 8, 7, 5, 5, 5, 4, 4, 3, 3, 2, 2, 2, 2, 1, 1, 1.

What comment would you make about the efficiency of this test?

2 In order to reduce the time taken up by examinations, a headteacher instructs his staff that, in future, examinations will consist of a half-hour test for each subject and will be held only once a year. What are the implications of this decision? How would it affect the individual teacher's assessments?

3 A teacher of mathematics sets a regular 20-minute test each week to his junior forms in order to reinforce the material which has been learned. Would it be acceptable simply to total these marks at the end of the term instead of setting an examination?

4 A history teacher has given a series of lessons on the origins of the Second World War, concentrating on the complex interaction of social, political and economic factors: the effects of the Treaty of Versailles, the Weimar Republic, inflation, the rise of Nazism, *lebensraum*, etc. He then sets a discriminating attainment test consisting of 30 short-answer questions of the following type:

1. Give the date of the occupation of the Ruhr by French forces.
2. What is the name given to the first attempt by the Nazis to gain power?
3. What was the name of the finance minister who succeeded in stabilizing the currency?

What comments would you make on the validity and reliability of this test?

Assignments

1 Define a unit of your teaching programme and draw up a specification for a test to be administered during one lesson period. Give examples of the type of question you would use and show how these test attainment of the objectives you have specified.

2 Taking the test devised for **1**, show what aspects of your course are *not* tested by it. Suggest other types of assessment that might be appropriate.

Suggestions for further reading

On objective tests

MACINTOSH, H. G. and MORRISON, R. B. *Objective Testing.* University of London Press, 1969.
(A useful and non-technical introduction to the subject.)

Most of the standard works on educational testing contain a section on objective tests (and much more besides); the following are recommended as useful reference books:

EBEL, ROBERT L. *Essentials of Educational Measurement.* Prentice-Hall, 1972.

THORNDIKE, ROBERT L. and HAGEN, ELIZABETH. *Measurement and Evaluation in Psychology and Education.* John Wiley, 1969.

VERNON, PHILIP E. *The Measurement of Abilities.* University of London Press, 1972.

(All three are extremely comprehensive and, it is fair to warn readers, deal at times with some fairly complex statistical procedures; Vernon probably goes into most detail on this score, and a fairly sound basis in mathematics would be necessary to get full value out of this work. For non-specialists, Ebel's book is probably the most straightforward and the book by Thorndike and Hagen is so encyclopedic that, even omitting the statistical sections, much of value remains.)

III. School examinations – written papers

In Chapter I, we defined an examination as a test, or a combination of tests and perhaps other assessment procedures as well. As far as written examinations are concerned, therefore, the points made in Chapter II regarding the construction of a single test apply also to the design of a whole examination. In this chapter, we shall consider first the application, to the broader field of a school examination, of those principles already discussed, then look briefly at teaching objectives before moving on to considering some examining techniques and the problems of marking the papers.

Planning an examination

Content validity must still be placed first on our list of requirements and a similar method to that suggested in Chapter II – an examination specification – can be adopted to achieve it.

The problems are similar, though bigger: aims and objectives, syllabus content, balance, etc. must be considered not just in relation to a relatively small part of the course but over a whole term or perhaps over a whole year. It must be remembered, though, that not all teaching aims can, or should, be examined; it may be a valid aim of a course, say, in civics, to make better citizens (however this is defined) but it is not going to be possible to say whether this has been achieved until ten or twenty years later, if then. On the other hand, an aim of the English department may be to ensure that no child leaves the school unable to read and write; this can certainly be measured, and should be.

Generally, however, with school examinations, we are likely to be concerned with the more limited and more clearly defined teaching objectives, with skills, abilities and knowledge, and it is in these terms that we should attempt to draw up the specification. But because we will probably have to assess a wider range of skills and cover a broader area of the curriculum than was the case with the classroom test, the specification must also be more elaborate.

To illustrate the way in which a range of techniques can be drawn upon to assess different aspects of the course, we shall take as an example a specification for a fifth-year examination in local studies (see Table 3). In this case, the teacher has designed an interdisciplinary course including elements of sociology, urban geography and applied science, focusing on the town in which the school is situated. The course is taken by pupils of a wide range of ability, though mainly

Table 3 Examination specification for a fifth-year local studies course (weightings are given as percentages)

Ability being assessed	Paper 1(a) (short-answer test)	Paper 1(b) (structured questions)	Paper 2 (essay paper)	Practical test (assignments)	Weighting
Knowledge of facts	15 (30 questions)				15
Interpretation of diagrams, maps, tables, etc.		10			10
Application of knowledge, skills, to simple problems, new situations, etc.		15 (4 questions of 5 parts)	20 (2 questions)		35
Ability to make observations, measurements, etc.				10	10
Ability to record results				10	10
Ability to interpret results			10 (1 question)	10 (oral)	20
Weighting	15	25	30	30	100

intending to leave school at the end of the fifth year, and has a fairly generous allocation of time.

In this course, the simple committing to memory of facts is not considered of major importance and greater emphasis is given to the application of knowledge; only 15 per cent is allowed in the short-answer test* for factual recall while in Paper 1(b) and in the essay paper it is the ability to interpret data and to apply what has been learned which is important.

The term 'structured questions' means questions set in the form of several sub-questions, all relating to the same topic, and usually forming an incline of difficulty, so that the later parts test higher-level skills than the earlier ones. In the second part of Paper 1, information in the form of tables of statistics, graphs,

---

* Short-answer tests (and most of the other types referred to in Chapter II) can be designed to test other abilities besides factual recall, of course.

maps and diagrams is presented on the paper; the use of structured questions allows the teacher to start with some fairly straightforward sub-questions and to progress to those requiring more sophisticated interpretations and the application to new situations of skills developed during the course – the more difficult parts carrying more marks than the earlier sub-questions.

In the third part, two essay questions are set to give the pupils the opportunity to develop arguments, to analyse, to discuss and to present points of view. There is a contrast between this part of the examination and the preceding one; here, the pupils have to draw upon their own knowledge in order to support and develop their theses and so the actual importance of factual knowledge is greater than the 15 per cent weighting on the specification grid would suggest. However, the emphasis here is on the use of facts, and it is the ability to select relevant information to use in the essay which is important.

In the third essay question, the ability to interpret the results of a survey, or other data, is being tested. This overlaps to some extent with Paper 1(b), but here a more complex analysis is being called for and less guidance in the form of the question structure is given; pupils are expected to work out their own interpretation and present reasoned arguments to support it.

The practical test takes the form of an assignment, where the pupil is given a simple investigation to carry out, such as a small-scale traffic survey, a study of some aspect of the welfare services, or the local water supply, etc., which has been a topic during the course. First, pupils have to decide on the method of tackling the problem and this is discussed with the teacher, who can guide the pupils with advice and suggestions where necessary. It is essential to allow for direction at this stage since shortcomings here would affect the subsequent investigations, but because of the difficulty of estimating just how much help has been given, no assessment is made.

The ability to carry out the assignment and to record the results are each the subject of assessments weighted at 10 per cent and the final assessment is an oral discussion (also 10 per cent) of the results with the pupil. An oral assessment is preferable here since it allows greater flexibility to adjust to the actual work done by each pupil.

It should be pointed out that it is not necessary for the practical test to be carried out at the same time as the written examination; indeed, since the assignments arise out of the work done during the course, it is more natural if they are undertaken as the opportunity occurs, though careful planning will have gone into the course beforehand to make sure that suitable occasions do arise.

In this scheme of examination, the teacher has attempted to give opportunities to his best pupils to use their ability while still offering reasonable chances to the less able. Remembering that the examination is a combination of several discriminating attainment tests, the purpose is to discriminate across the whole of the ability range; thus, Paper 1(a) will probably be most successful at distinguishing between lower levels of ability, while in Paper 2 the high-flyers can show what they can do.

To ensure validity, the teacher has arranged for the different aspects of the course to be reflected in the various components of the whole examination, each part of which is intended to test something different from the others. This is important: examining time is not to be squandered and there is little point in repeatedly testing the same abilities unless the test is so unreliable that repeated measurements are essential. It is also fair to give pupils, whose individual talents may be better suited to one part of the course than another, a chance to show where they can shine.

Finally, we would repeat the warning given in Chapter II that this is in no sense an ideal specification and that content validity must be judged in relation to each individual teacher's aims and syllabus. Just as each teacher is responsible for choosing a course of instruction which is suited to the needs and abilities of his own pupils, so is it necessary for each teacher to devise a scheme of assessment to suit that course.

Identification of teaching objectives

We have stressed the importance of the clear specification of the teacher's objectives, since they should dictate both the syllabus and the assessment. It is recognized, however, that it is by no means an easy task and that it may involve calling into question many activities which have become hallowed by long tradition. This, in itself, we would argue, is not necessarily a bad thing, nor should the fact of questioning mean that one expects always to get a negative answer; but because it is difficult, we would wish to interpolate here a short section on the identification of teaching objectives.

Pressure of space will not permit anything more than an outline, and, in any case, this is very much an area where each teacher must think things out for himself; we would hope to do no more than to indicate some possible lines of development.

The fundamental work in this field is Bloom's *Taxonomy of Educational Objectives** which has influenced almost every specification of objectives which

---

* *Taxonomy of Educational Objectives: the Classification of Educational Goals*, Handbook I: Cognitive Domain (Longmans Green, 1956); Handbook II: Affective Domain (Longmans Green, 1964).

has been produced in recent years. In Handbook I: Cognitive Domain, Bloom gives six major categories of objectives:

1 knowledge
2 comprehension
3 application
4 analysis
5 synthesis
6 evaluation.

These are in turn broken down into sub-categories. Each category includes those above it in the list – thus, application implies that the student must both possess certain basic knowledge and understand it before he can apply it.

Bloom's categories are very general and need to be interpreted in terms specific to particular subjects before they are of practical use in the context of examinations. Robert Ebel in *Essentials of Educational Measurement* (Prentice-Hall, 1972) classifies the abilities tested by examination questions into seven categories which can be summarized as follows:

1 understanding of terminology, or vocabulary
2 understanding of fact and principle, or generalization
3 ability to explain or illustrate (understanding of relationships)
4 ability to calculate (numerical problems)
5 ability to predict (what is likely to occur under specific conditions)
6 ability to recommend appropriate action (in some specific practical problem situation)
7 ability to make an evaluative judgement.

Not all of these will necessarily be appropriate to every subject.

There have been numerous statements of teaching objectives in different subjects (particularly in the sciences) but it would be impractical to try to give examples here. Rather we would stress again that, although one may find other people's views enlightening and helpful, it is ultimately part of the teacher's professional responsibility to select objectives which are appropriate to his particular group of pupils, and to specify those objectives in such a way that they can guide the construction of the syllabus and assessment.

To this end, Robert Thorndike and Elizabeth Hagen in *Measurement and Evaluation in Psychology and Education* (John Wiley, 1969) list eight characteristics which statements of objectives should have if they are to be operationally useful. These can be summarized as:

1 Objectives should be stated in terms of student behaviour, not in terms of learning activities or purposes of the teacher.

2　Objectives should begin with an active verb that indicates the behaviour a student should show in dealing with content. This format tends to guarantee a focus on the student and what he does.

3　Objectives should be stated in terms of *observable* changes in student behaviour.

4　Objectives should be stated precisely, using terms that have uniform meanings.

5　Objectives should be unitary; each statement should relate to only one process.

6　Objectives should be stated at an appropriate level of generality, not so general as to be meaningless nor so narrow that the educational process seems to be made up of isolated bits and pieces.

7　Objectives should represent intended direct outcomes of a planned series of learning experiences. It is common to find statements of objectives that deal with attitudes in programmes in which no particular instructional effort is given to the development of attitudes.

8　Objectives should be realistic in terms of the time available for teaching and the characteristics of the students.

As an illustration, we give an extract from *Measurement and Evaluation in Psychology and Education* (p. 263) of part of a specification of objectives for teachers of reading in an American school:

FUNCTIONAL READING ABILITIES

A　*Knows how to locate information*
　　1　Knows how to alphabetize
　　2　Knows how to use guide words
　　3　Knows how to use pronouncing key and diacritical marks
　　4　Knows how to use table of contents, index, glossary, appendix, preface
　　5　Knows how to use encyclopedia and other reference works

B　*Functional comprehension skills*
　　1　Knows specialized vocabulary
　　2　Applies reading skills to textbook materials
　　3　Develops specialized reading skills
　　　　(a) Interprets maps
　　　　(b) Interprets graphs and tables
　　　　(c) Interprets diagrams

C   *Uses organizing skills that aid in remembering what is read, such as:*
1   Classifying information
2   Analysing related items in sequence
     (a) Chronologically
     (b) In order of importance
3   Summarizing material
4   Preparing outlines
5   Taking notes
6   Formulating meaningful questions

D   *Remembers what is read*
1   Reports what has been read
2   Answers specific factual questions
3   Identifies sequence and relationships.

These summaries inevitably omit much of value in the originals; readers are recommended to consult the complete versions in the works which have been referred to.

We tried, in Chapter I, to show how the teacher's objectives should shape the content of the syllabus and hence the scheme of assessment; there can be cases, however, where the syllabus content may be non-existent or at any rate not determined in advance. A teacher who is following the Schools Council/Nuffield Humanities Curriculum Project, for example, would certainly wish to allow the course to develop according to the particular interests and abilities of his group of pupils since this is the philosophy on which the whole programme is based. In such a case, if an assessment is to be made at all, it can only be specified in terms of objectives, and the importance of the identification of objectives is underlined.

There are two further points that we should mention here: first, that sometimes people feel that if things are spelled out in the sort of detail that we have been advocating, something is lost and the teaching process becomes too mechanized and inhuman. We would agree that the relationship between teacher and pupil is an intensely personal one and one that must be safeguarded at all times; without a good relationship, teaching is unlikely to be effective. Nevertheless, the word teaching implies that one is trying to teach *something* and it is hard to see how this can be done efficiently unless it is clear what that something is. We would not, of course, recommend that the pupils are confined rigidly to some sort of curricular straitjacket, nor that the teacher should adhere to his plan so devoutly that all flexibility to adapt to the changing classroom situation is lost. But children appreciate purposeful teaching, which leads to recognizable progress towards a realistic and worth-while goal, and sensible planning of the course should not in any way detract from the teacher's ability to hold the children's interest.

Secondly, when objectives have been specified, and the specification drawn up, this is by no means the end of the story. It is still possible to write bad questions to a good specification; we would refer readers again to the considerations of validity and reliability in Chapter II, and to the checklist given there on pp. 38–42. It is sometimes debatable exactly what abilities are being tested by particular questions; not only can the judgements of even experienced examiners differ as to whether a question is testing application or comprehension, but the same question can test different abilities with different pupils – for example, a maths problem may, for one child, require the application of all his mathematical ability to work it out from first principles, while another has been so drilled in the necessary procedures that it is a matter of rote learning.

This last point is more of a problem with external examinations, when question spotting and exam cramming can defeat the best intentions of the examiners; the teacher setting his own internal examination should be better able to test the particular abilities he considers important. Which brings us full circle: these abilities must be identified.

Examination techniques – written papers

In the section on planning an examination at the beginning of the chapter we looked at the specification for an examination and at the way in which different techniques were used in the various papers; we shall now consider these techniques in more detail.

Essay questions
Essay questions are sometimes referred to as free-response or open-ended questions, which are perhaps more useful terms for our purposes; the word essay carries implications of a formal academic exercise of fairly substantial length, but, as we indicated in Chapter II, any question which allows an answer of more than a few words is straying over into the essay-type question.

It is more helpful, therefore, to distinguish between controlled response (multiple choice, true/false, etc.), restricted response (short answer, sentence completion) and free response where the pupil has to organize the answer in his own words. The answers to a free-response-type question may therefore vary in length from a sentence to a paragraph to, at an advanced level, essays of many pages, taking perhaps three hours to write.

The fact that the pupil has to answer the free-response question in his own words is at once the strength and the weakness of this technique. Strength, because it can allow the pupil to show creativity, a grasp of the wholeness of a topic, the depth and scope of his knowledge and his ability to organize his thoughts with coherence and relevance. Weakness, because it demands a level of writing skill which may or may not be adequately matched to the pupil's understanding of the subject, because the physical act of writing at any length takes time (thus reducing the number of questions which can be answered, which may affect validity), and because marking the answer is complicated by the mixing of two factors: subject attainment and writing ability.

The free-response question must be used with discretion. It is wasteful to ask pupils to write a half-hour essay which consists of nothing more than connecting facts which could be more efficiently tested by short-answer questions. Yet one analysis of examination papers in science* showed that in many cases, 90 per cent or more of the questions were testing no more than basic knowledge; while no one would deny that a sound basis of factual knowledge is essential in many subjects, not least in the sciences, most teachers would hope to be able to go beyond this level and it is frustrating and unfair for the pupils if the examination tests only the lowest ability.

When we decide to use free-response questions, therefore, we must use them in such a way that we capitalize on their strengths, or, looking at the reverse side of the coin, minimize their weaknesses by restricting their use to situations in which none of the other techniques is appropriate.

The first and most obvious example is in English; it would be difficult to imagine any English course which did not place emphasis on writing ability and equally difficult to conceive of any test of this ability except the essay or composition paper. Similarly, in many subjects in the humanities area, history, social studies, geography, etc., it will be mainly through essay questions that pupils have the opportunity to discuss, to analyse cause and effect and to argue a case. In most subjects, in fact, there will be some aspect of the course where the ability to give a clear account of an experiment, to write a report or to give instructions in writing will be important; in many occupations after leaving school, such ability will be highly valued and so there is a more general educational justification for including essay-type tests in school examinations. These considerations, however, reinforce the view that the essay should be used with care and essay subjects must be set in such a way that they do, in fact, elicit the abilities which it is desired to test.

The completely open subject, which may be little more than a title, is a double-edged weapon. With creative writing in English, it may be desirable to include topics such as The Caravan which can allow an imaginative child free rein to develop a story in virtually any way he wishes; there may be a penalty to be paid, though, with less creative pupils, and the prosaic list, "There are many different

* J. F. Eggleston, *A Critical Review of Assessment Procedures in Secondary School Science* (Leicester University Press, 1965).

57

kinds of caravan . . .' can become fairly disheartening if encountered in large numbers. Most teachers would therefore insist on giving some choice of essay subjects (though unfortunately not all children are wise enough to choose the topics to which they are best suited) and this is certainly an area where a choice of questions can be justified, in spite of the problems associated with this (see Chapter II, pp. 38–9). In addition to the open essay subject, most English examinations usually include some topics where more guidance on the appropriate treatment is given or where use is made of stimulus material in the form of a leading paragraph for discussion or perhaps a picture or some other non-verbal stimulus. In some cases, the distinction is carried further, and one section of the paper contains subjects which require an imaginative treatment while another is restricted to the factual kind of writing. (At the end of this chapter, we have included an example of an essay paper set for a public examination which illustrates some of the different types of essay subject.)

It must be recognized, however, that English is a special case; the stress is mainly on writing skill and, while the content of the essay is not unimportant, it is largely at the discretion of the pupil what that content is, and it is unlikely that the content of any two essays (particularly if there is a choice of subject) will be very similar. Neither is it likely to be the case in English essays that the content could be 'wrong' in the sense that factual errors would seriously affect the final mark; it is more probable that the essay would be graded mainly on the adequacy of the pupil's writing, on his ability to put across the ideas he wanted to, with less emphasis on what those ideas were.

This will not be so in other subjects, where the factual accuracy of the content is important, where there will be a certain amount of common ground (at any rate, in so far as all the essays will be historical or geographical, etc.) even between essays on different subjects, and where writing ability is important not as an end in itself, but as a means of conveying ideas about the subject being studied; provided that the quality of the writing is not so poor as to obscure communication, it is the quality of the ideas which will be the main basis for grading the essays. Even in such a case, however, the use of the quite open essay subject can be questioned. Not only can a subject such as 'Discuss the growth and importance of railways in Britain' present the pupils with considerable problems of selection and organization, but there is the additional risk that advantage may be taken of the open nature of the subject which is to some pupils a positive invitation to bluff and to flannel. This is sometimes done with considerable skill and some pupils can use their sophisticated command of essay-writing techniques to conceal very real shortcomings in knowledge of the subject. Admittedly, this is most likely to occur at fairly advanced levels and the crude attempts made by most school pupils can usually be spotted by the teacher; nevertheless, it would seem desirable to discourage even the attempt.

It may also be felt that the ability to tackle such a vague topic as that given in the example above is one which should be expected only at a very advanced level indeed; the development of the railway system is a topic worth a major historical study. Faced with such a subject to be answered in half an hour or so, the better pupils will be struggling with the problems of what to leave out and the weaker ones will be hard put to it to find something to fill the space. Under these circumstances, the teacher marking the question has only himself to blame if he finds, on the one hand, important points missed out, and on the other, irrelevancies and padding. It is, however, unfair to the children to penalize them for not doing what the examiner wanted, if he has failed to make this clear – which is another way of saying that the validity of this type of question may be suspect.

This leads, therefore, to the conclusion that matters will generally be improved by using the guided essay question* rather than a completely open subject:

> Describe the way in which children were employed in the textile industries in 1800.
> What controls were introduced in the next fifty years by the Factory Acts? How effective were these controls?

This question has two basically descriptive parts and a third element requiring some evaluation; because the different parts of the question are set in fairly specific terms, there is a much clearer directive to the pupils on how to tackle the question and it is also much harder to bluff one's way through. In this respect, the guided question may in fact be harder than the open essay – harder, and at the same time fairer, because it allows the children who really know the answer to demonstrate this.

It will usually be an improvement if the essay subject presents an unfamiliar problem or uses material organized in an unfamiliar way; we need the essay to discover the pupil's ability to use the information he has acquired, so we must place him in a situation where he has to do more than just reproduce by rote what has been learned in the classroom or from the textbook.

The following question, for example, tests little more than the ability to memorize:

> Describe in detail how you would determine (*a*) the solubility of sodium chloride in water at room temperature; (*b*) the mass of zinc which would react with 1 dm³ of molar hydrochloric acid.

(Moreover, although the question is in two parts, there is no real connection between them; they appear to have been put together simply in order to make an answer of equivalent length to that for some other question.)

* Sometimes referred to as multi-part questions or paragraph questions: also similar in many ways to structured questions – see pp. 61–3.

The ability to communicate is obviously as important for the science pupil as for the child studying any other discipline; the scientist must learn how to use prose accurately and concisely, and, in addition, must be able to illustrate his answers, where necessary, with diagrams, graphs, etc. The essay subject in the sciences must therefore be set so as to invite the exercise of all the communication skills needed, and, in addition, require the application of these skills to a novel situation, if the mere repetition of previously learned material is to be avoided.

If guided essay questions are used, there will be a gain in the discriminating power of the test if the different parts of the question can be arranged so that they call for the exercise of different abilities. This is particularly important if pupils of a wide range of ability are taking the same paper; in order to be able to distinguish both the highest and lowest levels of attainment, we should try to offer opportunities for all pupils to show what they can do. An example follows of a question in geography which attempts to achieve this sort of structure:

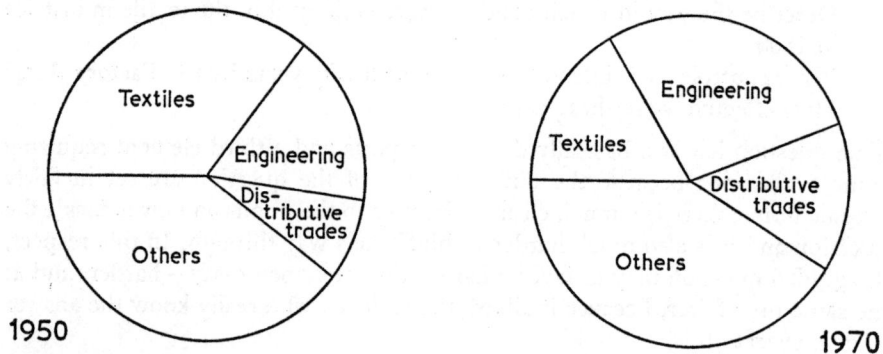

1950

1970

Employment in a Lancashire town in 1950 and 1970
(Distributive trades include mail-order firms, wholesale warehouses, etc.)

Study the two pie-charts above.

a   Name three trades that would be included under 'Others' on the charts.
b   Has the proportion of people working in the textile industry gone up or down since 1950? What reasons could you suggest for this?
c   Although a big increase is shown in employment in engineering, many firms have not found it necessary to build new factories. What would account for this?
d   'The Lancashire textile industry is no longer simply the cotton industry it used to be.' Explain the meaning of this statement.

Unless there is a very strong reason for setting an open essay subject, it appears that we shall gain considerable advantage from making the free-response question rather less free. In the next section, we shall look at structured questions, which take the points we have mentioned even further. In fact, of course, the dividing line between guided essay and structured question is by no means clear; structured questions tend to include one or two parts which may need no more than a few words to answer and often are based largely on material provided in the paper. However, definitions and practice vary widely and the theoretical distinctions are not very important.

Structured questions
Structured questions are well suited to meet two of the criteria which we mentioned in the preceding section: they can be arranged to test different levels of ability in the different sub-questions and they can test pupils' ability to cope with unfamiliar material or problems.

   If an examination specification has been drawn up, it may be advisable to try to match the sub-questions to the specification of abilities to be tested, though it would be unwise to allow oneself to be too rigidly confined by this and, of course, in some cases it will not be possible. If the questions are structured in this way, they will in effect form an incline of difficulty, so that the pupil is being asked to perform tasks of increasing complexity as he works through the question. An alternative approach is to aim each sub-question at a different aspect of the problem so that the various factors in it are isolated and dealt with one at a time. Or some combination of these two methods may be appropriate.

   However the sub-questions are to be arranged, there are certain points which should be observed:

i   *If material is provided to form the introductory part of the question, it should be selected with great care.*
The suitability of the introductory material for a structured question is vitally important. Wherever possible, a variety of material – written, maps, diagrams, photographs, etc. – should be used, not only to avoid the risk of boredom for the pupils, but because it is more likely that the various skills and abilities developed in the course will be covered if material of different types is used. It eases the problems of finding suitable material if the habit is developed of keeping an eye open throughout the year so that a stock is gradually accumulated which can be drawn upon at examination time.

ii   *Introductory material should contain no more than is relevant to the questions to be asked.*
The material should be edited so that superfluous matter is removed. Time is wasted reading through unnecessary words but this point also applies to maps,

diagrams, etc. where irrelevant details can confuse the children, distract them from what is being tested and so reduce validity.

iii *Sub-questions should be independent, though related to the main theme.*
This is essentially the same point that was made in Chapter II, p. 40. It can be more difficult, however, with structured questions, since the subject-matter is common to all the sub-questions; particularly when calculations are involved, it can be extremely difficult to avoid making the more complex operations dependent on the successful solution to the earlier parts. Nevertheless, it is vital that this is done, otherwise one of the main reasons for using structured questions is defeated, and the same effect could be achieved by a single question involving several steps.

An example follows of a structured question in mathematics,* which aims to test different levels of interpretation of the graph and the ability to make some calculations from the data given.

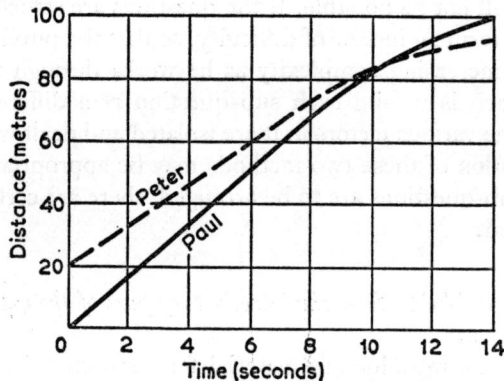

The diagram shows the graphs of two runners Peter and Paul in a 100-metre race.

- **a** What handicap was Peter allowed?
- **b** How much further had Paul run than Peter by the time that the race ended?
- **c** When and where did Paul overtake Peter?
- **d** What ratio did Peter's average speed bear to Paul's average speed?
- **e** How far did each runner go before he started to slow down?

* Adapted from Examinations Bulletin No. 1, *The Certificate of Secondary Education: Some Suggestions for Teachers and Examiners* (HMSO, 1963), p. 61.

It will be seen from these remarks that there is no special mystique about structured questions; basically, the same sort of approach is used as for writing short-answer questions for a classroom test, but with the extra complications of grading the sub-questions and relating them to a single theme. The whole operation is in fact very like setting a short test on a single topic, using questions which may vary from the restricted-response type to something verging on a short essay subject.

Comprehension passages

Passages in English and modern languages on which questions are set to test comprehension can be regarded as a special case of the structured-question technique; there is the similarity that an introductory paragraph is given, followed by questions, often of varying difficulty. However, there is a major difference: an important aspect of linguistic comprehension is the ability to identify relevant information which is buried away in the middle of a passage, and so it will probably be considered advisable not to edit the passage as severely as was recommended above. This must not be carried too far, of course – it is still a waste of examining time to ask children to read through twenty lines or so in order to answer a single question (unless it is a very important question indeed, and is weighted accordingly).

The difficulty of comprehension tests can be varied by the difficulty of the passage itself, or by the difficulty of the questions. Since one is trying to test comprehension of the passage, it is advisable to keep the questions fairly straightforward in wording, but questions which require understanding of the whole of a passage to answer are usually more searching than those which can be answered by studying only a sentence or two. Bearing in mind the need to choose a passage which is at least to some extent understandable by pupils of varying abilities, it will probably be most satisfactory if a text is chosen which contains some sort of an incline of difficulty (or a series of peaks of difficulty) within it.

We are considering the comprehension test as part of a whole scheme of examination, not in isolation. Since we assume, therefore, that essay writing, oral work, etc. will be tested in another part of the examination, it is important that the comprehension test should test only comprehension, and as far as possible avoid relying on written skills to show how far the passage has been understood. Taken to its furthest, this argument means that we would test reading comprehension by an objective test, so that reading (and selecting the answer) is the only ability involved. In view of the difficulties of constructing an objective test, which we referred to in Chapter II, most teachers would probably wish to use short-answer or sentence-completion questions instead. It is probable that the loss of validity will be small if the amount of writing is kept to a minimum, and if, when it is essential that several words or a sentence are given in the answer, the marks are awarded on the content of the answer, not on the style, spelling, grammatical accuracy or whatever. It may be difficult to accustom oneself to giving high marks to an answer which is very poorly expressed, but we should remember that written expression will be better tested in the composition paper, where virtue will be rewarded, and that the comprehension test may be the only place where understanding of the written word is tested to a significant extent. If comprehension is considered to be an important ability, then we should try to test it on its own – as an extreme example, two children may be equally incapable of writing a coherent sentence, but one may be much better at understanding than the other; a comprehension test which involves a lot of writing may be unable to distinguish between the two.

There may be occasions where more than just comprehension is involved; for example, in English literature, the teacher may be interested as much in the child's response to a poem, and in the way in which he expresses that response as in the more bread-and-butter question of understanding, in the sense in which we have been using the word. This is quite a different matter, much more like providing a stimulus for an essay than a comprehension test, and it would, of course, be appropriate to use open-ended questions. But because it is different, there would still be a place for the comprehension passage in the whole examination.

Précis or summary

The ability to identify the main points in a passage, or to follow the course of an argument, is undoubtedly involved in précis writing and is equally an important and useful skill. However, the rather artificial restrictions with which the exercise is often hedged about ('Tell the story in your own words . . . not more than 80 words') seem to serve no very clear purpose. It would seem quite possible to ask the children directly to list the main points in the passage, or to arrange a series of questions to this end, so that the exercise becomes much more like a comprehension test, but without the irrelevant problems of trying to find one's own words (for something which may have already been expressed perfectly adequately in the original) and the arbitrary limitation on the number of one's own words that may be used. It is a matter for some regret that more attention has not been given to *aural précis*. The ability to summarize the salient points of a discussion, or to make meaningful notes from a talk or radio broadcast is obviously of great potential importance to the child (see Chapter IV, pp. 87–90).

Certificate of Secondary Education/1974

ENGLISH PAPER/I

(see pages 76–8)

For use with Question A3

For use with Question B5

For use with Question B6

(a)

(b)

For use with Question B7

(a)

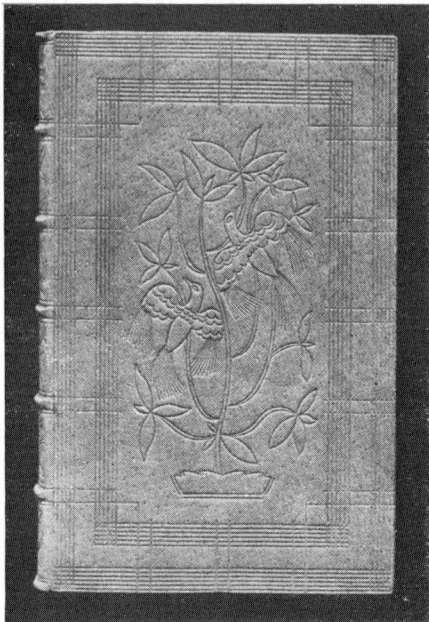

(b)

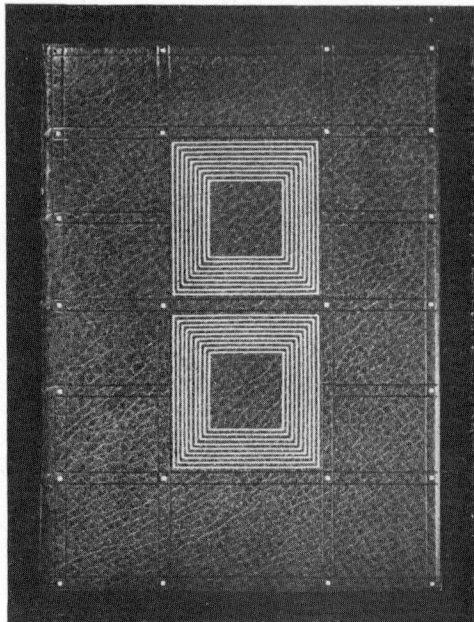

(c)

For use with Question C9

(b)

(a)

Translation etc.

Translation into English from a foreign language could be described as a comprehension test with complications; the original text has to be understood, with the subsequent task of expressing this understanding in a way that, ideally, conveys both the meaning and something of the flavour of the foreign language original. However, consideration of this and other matters related to modern language testing (translation into the language, dictée, etc.) are too specialized for inclusion in a general introductory book such as this and teachers of modern languages are referred to some of the standard works listed at the end of the chapter.

Open-book examinations – prepared questions

In an attempt to cut down the importance of memory in examinations, some experiments have been carried out with open-book tests, where pupils are allowed to use textbooks, notes, etc. in the examination. To try to reduce the strain of examinations, and to eliminate the chance factor, the system of prepared questions has also been tried out.

a *Open-book examinations*
So far, the results of experiments have not been very encouraging; in fact, the availability of the textbook appears to make little difference to the performance of the best pupils (who are usually also the quickest readers and the most skilful in using books) while the weaker children may waste a lot of time in a fruitless search for information and may also be tempted into unselective copying.

Nevertheless, there is still a need for more experimentation; it is possible, for example, that the inconclusive results mentioned may have been due to the fact that the children had been trained not to use books in the examination and, with the appropriate preparation, things might have been different.

It could also be argued that the skill of finding information quickly is an important one, perhaps just as important as the ability to remember particular facts. In this case, however, we would think that the skill could be better assessed during the course, when many more sources are available, rather than in an examination.

There are some important exceptions to the above remarks: the ability to use an atlas is obviously important to the geographer and the practice of supplying atlas extracts, or permitting the use of atlases in geography examinations is now fairly common. This is not an exact parallel with, say, the use of a chemistry textbook, because the interpretation of maps is a particular and important skill which many geographers would hold is worth testing in its own right; more similar would be the use of a dictionary in a modern language examination, though this is rare at present, or the use of lists of formulae etc. in mathematics, so that the examination tests understanding and application without being also a test of the ability to memorize.

b *Prepared questions*
If the subjects of essay questions are released some time before the examination, pupils can prepare their answers beforehand. This allows for a period of well-motivated study but there is also a risk that the children may delay all serious effort until the topics are available. The method also seems liable to encourage children to attempt to learn complete answers by heart, perhaps without any real understanding, and is also open to the objection that the period of examination tension is spread over a longer time.

If prepared questions are used, we would recommend that they should be supplementary to a more conventional essay test and other examination procedures.

Marking written papers

Most of the problems of marking the classroom test can be taken care of in the setting of the test, by careful arrangement of the paper, by wording the questions so that the possible range of answers is restricted, and so on. By such means, we can ensure a reasonably objective standard of marking, but when we consider the marking of free-response-type papers, the problems are much more difficult.

It is mainly a question of reliability: we must try to make sure that any paper would get the same mark, no matter when or by whom it was marked.

Considering again the possible sources of variability, we can see that the marking may suffer from unreliability owing to:

i *Variations in the judgement of an individual marker*
Nobody is absolutely consistent; standards may change after an interruption, after marking a number of papers; external influences (health, noise, the effect of a meal) may cause an alteration in standards or the marker may be unconsciously affected by untidy writing, by poor spelling, or by personal feelings towards the particular child concerned (or, equally bad, a teacher may be aware of these dangers and over-compensate).

ii *Differences between several markers*
Even when steps have been taken to ensure that markers are in general agreement about the qualities which are to be looked for in the answers to the papers, opinions may differ as to the extent to which they are present in an individual script.

66

It is not possible to eliminate these sources of variability entirely, but we can go a long way towards reducing them.

i *Variations in the judgement of an individual marker*
Discussions with colleagues (as outlined in the following section, pp. 69–71), are a great help even when one person is responsible for marking all the papers, since it enables one to clarify the mind about the qualities to be looked for. Preparation of model answers is also a useful exercise and certainly a detailed mark scheme should be drawn up; it is in fact usually best if both these are done when the paper is being set, in which case provisional mark allocations can be given on the paper. These serve as a useful guide for the children as to the importance of the various questions.

We must attempt to make the marking as objective as possible and, wherever it is appropriate, the marking should be on a right or wrong basis – this can usually be achieved in a short-answer paper or in certain parts of a structured question. It must be remembered, though, that alterations have to be made to most mark schemes as the papers are worked through, and that in the light of the actual marking, one may find that an unexpected interpretation of the question has led to an answer that had not been anticipated; in such a case, the mark scheme must be amended and previously marked scripts should be checked in case the amendment causes credit to be given to previously rejected answers. Incidentally, it is advisable to try to arrange the mark allocations so that they correspond either exactly or in a simple proportion (half, twice, etc.) to the percentage weighting for the question. It is possible to scale a mark out of 19 to a weighting of 10 per cent but it introduces another source of error and it is better to avoid problems if possible.

In many parts of the paper, of course, a simple marking method will not be applicable and the construction of a mark scheme for essay-type questions is extremely complex. In most subjects, it is advisable to try to assess separately different aspects of the essay, since the essay will probably be used to test several objectives, not just one. Structured questions may often be dealt with in this way; if, for example, the first two or three sub-questions ask for factual information, they might be marked simply on factual accuracy, disregarding the quality of the writing, while in the later parts, requiring perhaps the development of some ideas, the manner in which they were expressed might also be taken into consideration.

In marking complete essays, it will be necessary to consider such matters in the context of the whole, and it may be possible to divide the total mark allocation for the question into various sub-headings, so much for accuracy of facts, so much for development of ideas, so much for quality of writing, etc. A valid division of this nature can only be made if the teacher is absolutely clear about what he wants to test in the essay and the questions are designed to that end. And even within the categories that have been thus established, there can be room for differing opinions (is 'I walked five mile to school' a grammatical error, a slip of the pen or an example of possibly effective dialect usage?) and for over-lap between categories (can you award marks for interpretation of facts, if the facts are incorrect?). In practice, therefore, no analytical mark scheme of this kind is foolproof nor can it be applied absolutely rigidly.

It can be extremely difficult also to reach a judgement on one aspect of an essay without being affected by the others, particularly by the quality of the writing; for this reason some people would prefer to grade essays by the method of total impression, rather than according to an analytical scheme. Impression marking, however, is very liable to suffer from the marker's own variability and it is best to use multiple marking if possible. If this cannot be done, then it is a good idea to choose a number of scripts to use as reference points. The number chosen depends on the mark scale being used but if we assume that the essays are to be marked out of 20, then about five scripts would be enough. After skim-ming quickly through the pile of papers to get an idea of the general standard, the teacher should choose five that represent a good spread of marks; these are then marked in detail. Supposing that the five scripts are given 17, 14, 11, 8 and 3, they are then retained for reference; the rest of the essays are given marks in relation to these five points, i.e. a little better than 3, but not nearly as good as 8, mark 4.

Depending on what use is to be made of the assessments, it may be found sufficient simply to arrange essays in order of merit, without assigning any marks. The rank ordering alone can provide useful information and, if desired, can later be divided into broad grades. It is essential that some form of grading is adopted if the assessments of the essays are to be combined with another component of the examination which has been given numerical marks; the marks will also produce a rank order which can be graded in similar fashion to the essays and the two sets of grades can be combined. There are difficulties in combining rank orders directly, which will be discussed further in Chapter V.

Even if essays are marked according to an analytical mark scheme or by im-pression, it is still a useful check if the scripts are physically placed in rank order after the marking is completed. By glancing quickly through the papers in order of merit, it can be seen whether the marking method has been working effec-tively and whether the 23rd essay is, in fact, better than the 24th.

Whatever method is adopted, it is important to make sure that the whole of the mark (or grade) scale is used. Sometimes one hears the view that a mark of 10 out of 10 should not be awarded because it represents perfection, and some teachers restrict themselves to a maximum of 8 marks out of 10. Of course, 10 out of 10 does not mean that a child knows everything about the subject, any more than 0 means that he necessarily knows nothing. What it does mean is that he has achieved the best performance likely on one particular question from one particular group of pupils; and that is precisely what 8 out of 10 means from a teacher who never gives more than this mark. There may be a case for not giving 0 (which is a fairly depressing mark for anyone to get) but it must be remembered that if a teacher never gives less than 3 or more than 8, this is effectively marking out of 6, not 10, and he might as well give marks from 1 to 6. But there is a danger that if the question is weighted at 10 marks, and all those marks are never in fact used, the other parts of the examination where the full mark range is used (the short-answer test, for example) may come to assume much more importance than was originally intended and the balance of the examination will be upset.

If it is possible, it is best to complete the marking of one set of questions in one session, though there comes a time when fatigue exercises an adverse effect and it is necessary to call a halt. When resuming after an interruption for whatever cause, it is wise to spend a little time reading through some previously marked scripts so as to remind oneself of the standard of marking. When the marking is completed, too, it is worth while checking back at random to see if there has been a drift of standards during the course of the whole operation; it is common enough to find that the earlier papers have been marked more severely than the later ones. If numbers are too great for all papers to be marked by a single teacher, a possible compromise is for each teacher to mark all the answers to one question. Some form of standardization (discussed in the following section and in Chapter V) is still necessary; otherwise, if marker X is severe and marker Y is lenient, the children who have given good answers to the question marked by Y will score better than those who have answered X's question well.

ii *Differences between several markers*

Where several teachers are involved in the marking, it will be necessary to adopt similar methods to those applied in an external examination to standardize the marking among a team of assistant examiners. In the school situation it is to be hoped that a greater degree of community of judgement would exist among colleagues in a department than with a team of markers recruited from many different sources, so a somewhat abbreviated procedure is suggested below.

The head of the department (or other teacher responsible for co-ordinating the marking) selects ten or a dozen scripts (making sure that they cover a range of ability) and marks them according to the agreed mark scheme. These are then circulated to other members of the department (or if possible, photocopied so that they may be retained for reference) and a departmental meeting is arranged at which the marking is discussed and if necessary the mark scheme is adjusted. If model answers have been prepared, the scripts can be compared with them but, in any case, the discussion should lead to the identification of those qualities which are to be rewarded in the children's answers.

Having reached agreement, marking can proceed; it is desirable to make provision for difficult scripts to be referred for a second opinion, and also for a random selection of each teacher's scripts to be re-marked by the head of the department; following this check, it may be found necessary to scale or otherwise adjust the marks of one or more teachers, using the methods suggested in Chapter V.

It may well be that if a department is fortunate enough to have a staff who have worked together for some years, this procedure can be omitted. However, we would give a warning that it is dangerously easy to assume that agreement exists simply because one knows one's colleagues well, and that it is wise to take steps to verify the assumption from time to time. With a newcomer, of course, the head of department will need to make sure that he has the chance to become familiar with the methods and standards of the school; in such a case, the head of department might well mark some scripts jointly with the new teacher as well as checking later to see that the marking has been consistent.

It is worth considering, in a little more detail, the ways in which markers may differ from one another. First, one teacher may consistently give higher or lower marks than another. This is called difference of *standards*. It can be detected by comparing the average mark given to the same set of scripts by the two teachers, and can be corrected simply by a straightforward scaling of marks. Secondly, even though the average mark may be the same, the range of marks used may be different; one teacher may be using the whole of the mark range (thus implying that he can detect considerable differences between the children) while another bunches the marks together. This is called difference of *discrimination*. And thirdly, teachers may agree on standards, and on discrimination, but may differ on the rank order in which they would place individual children – indicating lack of *conformity*.

Variations between markers on discrimination and conformity are much harder to correct than differences on standards; in extreme cases, a complete re-marking may be necessary. Nevertheless, total agreement cannot be expected and the difficulty often is to decide how much variation is acceptable. Readers are referred to Schools Council Examinations Bulletin No. 5* which gives details of how to arrange an 'agreement trial' and of various tests† which can be applied to marks in order to find out what sort of differences exist between markers and how important they are.

---

* *The Certificate of Secondary Education: School-based Examinations: Examining, Assessing and Moderating by Teachers* (HMSO, 1965), pp. 7–14.

† The tests are designed to be applied to a CSE scale of 5 grades plus an ungraded category. See Appendix B for methods of adapting to other scales.

The informal standardizing procedure outlined at the beginning of this section relies on the assumption that agreement among markers has been reached, and on the ability of the head of department to detect whether there has been any departure from the agreed standards by his scrutiny of sample scripts. In many cases, this may well be adequate but it would be advisable to remember two things: first, that it is not easy to reach an independent judgement about the quality of a piece of work if someone else's mark is imprinted on it and it is best if the first mark can be covered up during the checking process. Secondly, since it is not reasonable to expect complete agreement, a degree of judgement must be exercised as to whether differences are the normal variations which are inevitable, or whether they indicate a more serious disagreement. The advantage of the procedures given in Schools Council Examinations Bulletin No. 5 is that they offer a method of quantifying these differences according to certain criteria.

We referred to the advisability of obtaining a second opinion on scripts which prove difficult to assess; there is a considerable gain, particularly in subjects like English where marking must depend heavily on subjective judgement, if it can be arranged for all scripts to be multiple-marked. Obviously, this can present difficulties in organization and it would be worth while attempting to overcome these only in cases where the increase in reliability is significant, as has been found to be the case with English compositions. Several marking experiments have shown that using teams of three markers and totalling (or averaging) their marks gives a much more reliable score than that obtained from a single marker; even the combined marks of two markers is an improvement, though increasing the number of markers above three shows that the gain in reliability begins to flatten out. With multiple marking, it is usually expected that each marker can work more quickly, giving a rapid impression mark, so that the time taken up in the marking is not that much longer than a single marker would need – certainly not twice or three times as much – if two or three markers are used. But it is vitally important that the mark given by the first marker does not appear on the script, otherwise it will influence the other markers and the purpose of multiple marking is defeated.

Marking written papers – general points
We would advocate that marked scripts are returned to the pupils after the examination and that in addition to the actual marks there should be written or oral comments from the teacher to indicate where marks have been lost or gained, and how things can be improved next time. Without such feedback an important teaching opportunity is lost and it is hard to see how the children can be expected to do better if it is not explained where they have gone wrong. There is a subsidiary advantage in this procedure in that the pupils will inevitably make a very

71

careful check on the mechanical accuracy of the marking and addition of marks; this is an area where it is easy to make sometimes quite substantial slips and where it is advisable to have some form of checking. Thirty children can check thirty papers much more quickly than a single teacher and at examination time it is good to be relieved of a rather tedious, though necessary, chore.

There is one final matter that we should refer to in connection with marking and that is the insidious 'halo' effect. Halo effect means that one's judgement may be subconsciously affected by some extraneous factor, and because it is subconscious it is difficult to detect. Ways in which halo effect can operate are:

i judgement may be affected unduly by neat presentation, handwriting, etc. which gives an impression of competence which may or may not be reflected in the content (or the reverse – bad writing etc. may create an impression of ignorance);

ii the impression created by the first answer on the paper may carry over and influence the mark given to the next one, which may be much better (or worse);

iii marking may be affected by personal relationships (good or bad) between teacher and pupil.

Unfortunately, it is difficult to know whether one has been influenced in any of these ways or not, so it is best to adopt methods which are less susceptible to halo effect than others. Thus, as far as is possible, scripts should be treated as anonymous, that is, one should avoid looking at the names until marking has been completed (though it may be hard to avoid recognizing the writing). The adoption of a mark scheme as objective as possible should help to eliminate the effect of good or bad presentation and if each question is marked for all pupils (that is, all question 1s marked, then all question 2s, etc.), not only will it help to maintain standards of marking but it should prevent the carry-over of an impression from one answer to another.

Summary of Chapter III

The validity and reliability of the examination are matters of prime importance. A clear definition of objectives and of the syllabus, together with an examination specification, will help to ensure good validity. Reliability can be improved by careful setting of question papers and by adopting as objective a marking method as possible. Halo effect must be guarded against in any marking process.

Questions on Chapter III

(Outline answers are given in Appendix A.)

1 The aims of a course in general science are stated to be:

i   to develop the scientific way of thinking;
ii to encourage an interest in science generally;
iii to develop the ability to use scientific equipment;
iv to train pupils to make accurate observations and to interpret the results.

Which (if any) of these aims are stated in such a way as to indicate the sort of examination which should be set?

2 Example of comprehension passage and question:

> Text: 'Twas brillig and the slithy toves
> Did gyre and gimble in the wabe . . .'
> Question: What were the toves doing?
> Expected answer: Gyring and gimbling.

What is the question testing, if anything?

3 When marking a school examination, members of the English department are instructed to grade the papers in five broad categories – A, B, C, D, E. On the basis of this assessment, pupils will be divided into sets: A, for more advanced work; B, C, D, an average middle band; and E, a remedial set. What comment would you make on this procedure?

Assignments

1 a State the aims and objectives of your own teaching programme.
  b Which of these are assessable by written examination techniques?
  c How far do your aims and objectives match those of the external examination (if any)?

2 Prepare an examination specification for one year-group in your school.

3 Draw up an example of a structured question (or guided essay) in your subject. Show how the different parts of the question attempt to test different levels of ability.

4 Take a previously set question paper in your subject and prepare model answers and mark scheme.

5 If possible, obtain some samples of examination scripts (preferably essay-type questions).

a Mark these according to your preferred method. Record the marks, but do not write them on the paper. Re-mark after a period of time and compare results.

b As above, but circulate the scripts to be marked among a group of colleagues, after agreeing a mark scheme. Compare the results.

Suggestions for further reading

On techniques of assessment
(In general, but mainly in relation to public examinations.)

HUDSON, B. (ed.) *Assessment Techniques: an Introduction*. Methuen Educational, Education Paperbacks, 1973.
   (An extremely useful book.)
MACINTOSH, H. G. (ed.) *Techniques and Problems of Assessment*. Edward Arnold, 1974.
   (At a more sophisticated level.)

The Examinations Bulletins series contains much valuable material; a full list is given in the general bibliography at the end of the book, pp. 187–8. The following Examinations Bulletins are relevant to Chapter III:

1. *The Certificate of Secondary Education: Some Suggestions for Teachers and Examiners*. HMSO, 1963.
   (Worth reading for its sections on examining methods and the general philosophy of examinations.)
5. *The Certificate of Secondary Education: School-based Examinations: Examining, Assessing and Moderating by Teachers*. HMSO, 1965.
   (Deals with methods of comparing different assessors' judgements and estimating the significance of differences – see also Appendix B.)
12. *Multiple Marking of English Compositions: an Account of an Experiment* by J. N. Britton, N. C. Martin and H. Rosen. HMSO, 1966.
16. *The Certificate of Secondary Education: Trial Examinations: Written English*. HMSO, 1967.
   (These last two contain accounts of multiple-marking experiments.)

On modern language testing
DAVIES, ALAN (ed.) *Language Testing Symposium: a Psycholinguistic Approach* (Language and Language Learning Series). Oxford University Press, 1968.
   (Contains articles on various aspects of language testing both of modern languages in this country and of English for foreigners, as well as chapters on item analysis, objective testing, etc.)
LADO, ROBERT. *Language Testing*. Longmans Green, 1961.
VALETTE, REBECCA M. *Modern Language Testing: a Handbook*. Harcourt, Brace & World, 1967.
   (The last two are extremely comprehensive, though referring mainly to practice in the United States.)

Taxonomy of Educational Objectives
Two volumes of the *Taxonomy* have been published so far:

BLOOM, B. S. (ed.) *Taxonomy of Educational Objectives: the Classification of Educational Goals*, Handbook I: Cognitive Domain. Longmans Green, 1956.

KRATHWOHL, D. R., BLOOM, B. S. and MASIA, B. B. *Taxonomy of Educational Objectives: the Classification of Educational Goals*, Handbook II: Affective Domain. Longmans Green, 1964.
(Concerned with values, attitudes, interests, etc.)

A third volume, Psychomotor Domain, is to be published.

Example of an English examination essay paper *

Associated Lancashire Schools Examining Board
CSE English/Paper I (Written Expression)

Time allowed is 1½ hours. Answer **three** questions in all, choosing **one** from each section. Spend about half an hour on each question. You are allowed ten minutes in which to read the questions. During this time you are not allowed to write anything. Write your answers in the answer book provided. You may use a dictionary if you wish.

SECTION A

*In this section you are required to produce a vivid piece of writing on **one** of the following subjects.*

A1 Read carefully the poem printed below and with it in mind write an imaginative account of a season which especially pleases or displeases you.

> Cottonwool clouds loiter.
> A lawnmower, very far,
> Birrs. Then a bee comes
> To a crimson rose and softly,
> Deftly and fatly crams
> A velvet body in.
>
> A tree, June-lazy, makes
> A tent of dim green light.
> Sunlight weaves in the leaves,
> Honey-light laced with leaf-light,
> Green interleaved with gold.
> Sunlight gathers its rays
> In sheaves, which the wind unweaves
> And then reweaves – the wind
> That puffs a smell of grass
> Through the heat-heavy, trembling
> Summer pool of air.
>
> A. S. J. Tessimond

A2 Suppose that you have left your family to begin life on your own. Describe your feelings and experiences as you leave, **or** when you are away, **or** when later, for whatever reasons, you return.

---

* Photographs for use with the exam paper appear between pp. 64 and 65.

A3 Look carefully at the two photographs intended for use with this question. Write an account of what **one** of them means to you.

A4 Read carefully the poem printed below. Imagine that you are involved in **one** of the three kinds of warfare described in the poem: medieval **or** trench **or** atomic. Describe your experiences and feelings in that situation.

> There are many cumbersome ways to kill a man:
> . . . you can take a length of steel,
> shaped and chased in a traditional way,
> and attempt to pierce the metal cage he wears.
> But for this you need white horses,
> English trees, men with bows and arrows,
> at least two flags, a prince and
> a castle to hold your banquet in.
>
> Dispensing with nobility, you may, if the wind
> allows, blow gas at him. But then you need a mile of
>   mud sliced through with
> ditches, not to mention black boots, bomb craters,
> more mud, a plague of rats, a dozen songs
> and some round hats made of steel.
>
> In an age of aeroplanes, you may fly
> miles above your victim and dispose of him by
> pressing one small switch. All you then
> require is an ocean to separate you, two
> systems of government, a nation's scientists,
> several factories, a psychopath and
> land that no one needs for several years.
>
>   from Edwin Brock: 'Five Ways to Kill a Man'

SECTION B

In this section you should write as clearly and methodically as possible on **one** *of the following topics.*

B5 Describe in detail the kitchen/dining room shown in the photograph which accompanies this question and explain what advantages or disadvantages you think it has.

B6 Describe carefully the principal features of the design of the two cars shown in the photographs accompanying this question and explain their differences and similarities.

B7 Look carefully at the books photographed for use with this question. Describe them in detail making clear their differences.

SECTION C

In this section you are required to write persuasively, that is, to persuade someone to your point of view.

C8 Suppose that a place, subject or hobby in which you are particularly interested is shortly to be treated in a series of four or five TV programmes. Write an article suitable for the *Radio Times* or the *TV Times* encouraging viewers to watch the series.

C9 Both the photographs for use with this question are of swans. Write a letter to a newspaper on the evils of the pollution which has turned the birds into what they are in photograph (b) and befouled streams, rivers and coastlines of our country. (Omit addresses and begin your letter with 'Dear Sir. . .')

C10 Write persuasively to a member of your town council urging that recreational facilities for children in towns and cities be made better than those shown in the photograph for use with this question. (Omit addresses and begin your letter with 'Dear Sir. . .')

IV. Orals, practicals, projects – course-work assessment

In this chapter we shall consider some of the problems of oral examining, together with a brief discussion of aural tests. We shall then look at the assessment of practical work and projects, and finally at the assessment of course work, continuous assessment, and some of the problems of expressing assessments in terms of marks or grades.

Orals

Oral examinations are difficult to conduct, time-consuming and may be less reliable than written tests. Nevertheless, since the oral may be the only valid way of testing certain skills, the problems must be faced.

In modern languages, the importance of oral work hardly needs to be stressed nowadays, and in English teaching too there has been a growing realization that effective oral communication is as important as (or perhaps more important than) written work.

In these cases, the oral is used as a test of spoken language; however, in other subjects, oral techniques may be found to be advantageous as a method of examining since the examiner can use the flexibility of the oral to discuss matters in depth with an able pupil, to tease out the meaning of an obscure statement, to probe for the reasons for a conclusion – in effect, to test understanding, in the fullest sense, while retaining the ability to adjust the level of his questioning to children of higher or lower ability.

Some teachers have found, in fact, that in the oral situation, many children can achieve a higher standard of work than they can provide evidence of in written form; experience in the oral examining of history, for example, has shown that pupils who, from written answers alone, would have been classified as below average, can nevertheless develop and sustain historical arguments of some complexity in oral discussion. An interesting account of oral examining in chemistry is given in Examinations Bulletin 21, *CSE: an Experiment in the Oral Examining of Chemistry*. (See also the section on the assessment of practical work, pp. 94–6.) Oral assessments may be particularly valuable with mixed-ability groups, where some pupils' deficiencies in skills of reading and writing may invalidate the usual methods of testing attainment in many subjects.

In this country, we have hitherto relied almost exclusively on written examining techniques. It is to be hoped that teachers of all subjects will be encouraged to experiment with oral testing because it could be a valuable supplement to existing methods.

Problems of oral examining

i *Time*

The time taken to administer oral tests is one of the greatest problems, and one to which there is unfortunately no easy solution.

It is sometimes possible to conduct orals on a group basis, with perhaps four or five pupils together, but, depending on the nature of the subject, this may or may not be appropriate. There are obviously difficulties of assessment; one child may be excessively verbose and monopolize the discussion, another may be over-awed and contribute nothing. Group orals, therefore, make considerable demands on the teacher's skill in guiding the discussion so that each child has a fair chance; however, this does not mean simply that each child is allowed five minutes' speaking-time – obviously, if this were done, there would be little saving in time over individual five-minute tests. A child's participation in the discussion is not necessarily shown by the quantity of speech but rather by the quality. Even a monosyllabic interjection, if pertinent, may represent a more significant contribution than a lengthy oration, and show that the pupil has been following developments actively. It is important, however, that each child does make a contribution and that the assessment is based on some evidence; the child who sits in silence with furrowed brow may be thinking thoughts too deep for words but whether the thoughts are relevant to the topic under discussion is a matter for conjecture. Unless he speaks, no assessment of oral ability can be made, just as no mark can be given on a written examination to a candidate who hands in a blank paper.

The assessment of group orals is not an easy task, and, though it *can* be done, it is the sort of area where the only way of learning is by doing; it may be helpful to discuss matters with a colleague who has experience of the problems, or, better still, to observe him in action and to participate in the marking. (See also the section on marking the oral, pp. 83–7, for an example of the assessment of group discussion.)

If a group assessment is decided on, the way in which the groups are arranged is a question on which there is some debate. Some people feel that if the children are allowed to form themselves into their normal friendship groups, there is a risk that members of the group may be constrained by the roles which they have adopted within it – the group's buffoon, its tough guy, its leader. On the other hand, a random grouping may lead to the situation where a child of lower ability is in a group with several high-flyers and is overwhelmed by them – or, possibly stimulated by them to higher achievements! In the absence of any clear guidance that can be given, it is probably best if the teacher arranges the groups according to his knowledge of the pupils, separating known trouble-makers, allowing friends who work well with one another to remain together and arranging for a mixture of ability in each group.

Another way of reducing the impact of the oral tests on the timetable is to make assessments during the course – a form of continuous assessment. This does not reduce the time taken so much as spread it out, but it can allow for a greater variety of oral work and for more natural conditions than when a special test is held. It must be remembered, however, that this method implies that different pupils will be assessed on different occasions and that attainment will vary from the beginning of the term to the end. The effect of this will be lessened if a number of very short assessments is made, so that all the children can be assessed on similar work within a short time, during a single lesson, perhaps, or at most inside a week. What this procedure means is that a single test situation has to be fragmented into several separate pieces and careful consideration is needed on whether this reduces validity or not.

The question of validity is, as always, the crucial one and pressures of time must not be allowed to shorten the test to the extent that its validity suffers. Syllabus coverage may well be inadequate with a very short oral and, particularly in an individual test, children take some little time to settle down; confidence and performance often improve noticeably after a few minutes. As we have said before in a different context, if the test is worth doing at all, it must be done well, and adequate time (and preparation) must be allowed for the oral, as for any other sort of test.

ii   Conduct of the oral test

In any oral test situation – individual, group or course assessment – a matter of great importance is the amount of guidance given by the teacher. It calls for a nice judgement to decide when a pause is due to a pupil's collecting his thoughts (and when the teacher's intervention would be premature and penalize the child) or when it is due to inability to answer (when the teacher must supply the answer or move on to another topic in order to maintain the right pace).

Many children find an oral examination a considerable strain and nervous tension may impair performance. It is generally true that children who have had plenty of practice in oral work become much more confident, but it is important that the teacher puts the pupil at ease by a relaxed and friendly approach. The teacher's familiarity with the test material and his confidence in his own ability are major factors in allowing him to inspire a similarly confident attitude in the pupils, and this is again an area where experience counts for a lot.

It is generally best to avoid, as far as possible, commenting on the accuracy or otherwise of the child's answers during the test. Some fairly neutral, but encouraging remark, such as 'fine', is advisable before moving on, even if the answer has failed to score many points on the mark sheet. Obviously, if the correct answer has to be given before the next part of the test can be tackled, the teacher must correct errors, but in general it is less conducive to loss of confidence if the children are not made aware of a succession of blunders.

iii *Structure of the oral test*
Many moderators of internally assessed orals for public examinations would say that one of the most difficult problems they have to face is to adjust marks in cases where an inexperienced teacher has conducted an oral test badly and candidates have not had a proper chance to show their ability. Like the open-ended essay, the unstructured oral has potentially great strengths and great weaknesses: strengths, because a good examiner has unique opportunities to test understanding in depth; and weaknesses, because a poor examiner may talk too much, upset the candidate, allow him to dry up, or may intervene too quickly.

As with the essay, then, there may be advantages in structuring the oral to some extent so that in at least part of the test there are standard elements such as common questions for all candidates.* Such a feature will be particularly desirable in a large school: the problems of standardizing oral assessments among several teachers are much greater even than the not inconsiderable difficulties of standardizing the marking of written scripts.

It may be possible to introduce some form of oral structured questions, for example using common visual material (maps, pictures, a short text) together with set questions of varying difficulty. In modern languages, role-playing (where each pupil is given instructions as to the part he is to play in a short dialogue, the teacher taking the other part) may be arranged so that it is common to all teaching groups.

It is not essential that the whole of the oral test should be formally standardized in this way; indeed, it may be thought undesirable to do so since the flexibility of the oral would be reduced and some of its value lost. However, if even a part of it is so structured that one can be sure that it has been conducted and marked in reasonably similar fashion across all teaching groups, then the marks on this part can be used to scale marks on the other (unstructured) elements – or course-work marks – by a fairly simple process. This will be described in Chapter VI.

The scaling procedure can adjust differences in marking standards between several teachers in a department, but, of course, it can do nothing about a teacher

---

* Security is always a problem with oral tests; it may be advisable to try to devise groups of questions of similar difficulty so as to be able to ring the changes from time to time.

who has conducted the oral so badly that the test is invalid. In such a case, the only courses of action are to disregard the marks completely or to retest. Both are rather drastic steps and it would obviously be preferable to avoid the chance of such a situation arising. It is very desirable that the head of department should make sure that all his teachers have the opportunity of acquiring the necessary expertise in oral testing by discussion of tape-recorded sample material or by sitting in when an experienced colleague is working. It is also advisable that occasional checks are made when oral testing is in progress, or colleagues might exchange classes from time to time as a way of becoming acquainted with one another's standards. In the case of a newcomer, of course, the head of department might have to take over the oral testing of certain sets, at any rate in the initial stages.

iv   Marking the oral test

Many of the problems of oral marking can be overcome if the material is made permanent, i.e. recorded. The teacher does not have to contend with the problems of conducting the test and simultaneously assessing it, difficult interviews can be listened to again at leisure, a second opinion can be asked for* and sample material is available for departmental discussion.

Some teachers have misgivings about using a tape-recorder, either doubting their ability to handle the equipment or fearing that the children will be put off by the presence of the microphone. Recording of modern–language orals for external moderation has been standard practice with some examining boards for several years and experience has shown most of these fears to be unfounded. Although there are occasional technical difficulties, most recordings are at least audible and if the children are given the opportunity of making recordings in class (and it is a useful teaching device to play their oral work back to them) they soon get used to the microphone.

With recorded material, marking becomes much more like marking written papers and it is worth going to some trouble to secure this advantage. Nevertheless, we recognize the practical difficulties and also the limitations of the tape; assessment of group work may be difficult (unless videotape is available) as is the recording of course work unless a recorder is more or less permanently running in the classroom. Paralinguistic features such as gesture can be an important part of communication and again, unless videotape is used, it may be felt that too much is lost in recording to allow a valid assessment; much depends on the subject, though, and the tape-recording may still be of value as an aide-mémoire.

---

* We would refer readers to the work of A. P. Dyson in modern languages – *Oral Examining in French* (Modern Language Association, 1972). Dyson found that even experienced examiners were liable to sudden inconsistencies and he concluded that more reliable results would be obtained by multiple marking from tapes.

As an example of one way of tackling the problems of oral assessment, Table 4 shows a specification* for the assessment of group discussion in the Schools Council/Nuffield Humanities Curriculum Project. We have referred, in Chapter III, to the difficulties of assessing this type of work where there is no previously defined syllabus content; nevertheless, if the course is intended to develop certain abilities in the children, then an assessment can be made in these terms.

The specification sets out the abilities – relating the argument to the evidence, developing the discussion, not being deflected by irrelevancies etc. – and in each category, defines the extremes of good and bad.

The discussion is tape-recorded and transcribed; each pupil's contribution is then analysed and assigned a letter corresponding to one of the categories and a numerical mark from 5 to 1 according to whether it falls nearer to the plus or the minus end. Following this process, each child will have a number of assessments in various categories which can be used for several purposes: diagnostic information will be available as to where a pupil shows weakness, the results of several assessments over a year should give a good indication of progress, and the analysis of the group as a whole should provide the teacher with evidence as to the effectiveness of the materials used as a basis for the discussion. The assessments can also be combined at the end of the course to form the basis for grading for an external examination since the evidence in the form of the tapes and transcripts is available at all times for moderation.

The process of recording and transcription is obviously time-consuming and, though it might be thought worth while for a course where there was little or no written work, there remain cases where recording is not practicable and the marking has to be done on the spot. Prior discussion of criteria among the department is even more vital in such a case and, together with the other suggestions made in the section on the structure of the oral test, pp. 82–3, should help to achieve some uniformity and stability of standards.

Where course-work assessment comprises a number of very short assessments (as suggested in the section on the time taken for oral examining, pp. 80–1) there will be advantage in using also a very short mark scale which can be applied rapidly and consistently. For example, in monitoring work in a language laboratory, the teacher from the console can, in a comparatively short time, listen to a single repetition of the master tape by each pupil. Each repetition can be marked on a 3-point scale: 2, if it is virtually perfect, 0 if it is worthless and 1 if it is anywhere in between. The potential unfairness of marking on a single example will be counteracted by the large number of assessments which can be made over a term and this spread of the assessment should also cater for the pupils' progress during the course. Certainly, such a simple (or, some might say, crude) mark scale can be applied fairly consistently, though, to achieve reasonable

* Devised by J. Miller, Blakelaw School, Newcastle upon Tyne.

Table 4 Specification for the assessment of group discussion

Main area of comment	Key to symbols	Analysis of comments
The nature of evidence	I+	Relates argument to evidence, seeks confirmation from evidence, queries nature of evidence.
	I−	Ignores significance of evidence, argues unsupported case, accepts ambiguity in evidence.
The intellectual process of discussion	C+	Introduces a basic concept in exploration of the issue.
	C−	Fails to appreciate or react to the emergence of a new concept.
	E+	Enlarges concept by introduction of a new facet.
	E−	Diminishes concept by reference to irrelevant particulars or repetition of aspects already explored.
	S+	Synthesizes a common theme or argument from several related particulars.
	S−	Fails to appreciate the significance of a synthesis and reverts to previous particulars.
	L+	Shows a preference for argument sustained by logic; questions prejudiced attitudes; queries hearsay evidence.
	L−	Adopts a prejudiced position unsupported by evidence; refuses to weigh counter-evidence; quotes or accepts unverifiable evidence.
Value judgements and personal positions	R+	Identifies the main issue and resists movement away from it; queries irrelevance in argument or in detail.
	R−	Fails to grasp the main issue, introduces irrelevant details or deviations.
	U+	Shows understanding of others' points of view, tolerance of other interpretations, willingness to concede the validity of other conclusions.
	U−	Shows lack of understanding and rigidity of thought, unwillingness to evaluate other positions.
	P+	Makes a positive contribution, enlarging current theme, adding body and depth to the discussion but without breaking new ground.
	P−	Makes a negative contribution repetitive of previously expressed opinions.
	M+	Maintains and justifies position in face of opposition; adheres to own line of argument until fully explored; resists movement away from unresolved issues.
	M−	Abandons a justifiable position in face of opposition; easily diverted from own position by weight of popular opinion or interest.
	B+	Shows an appreciation of the relationship between opinion, behaviour and social situation.
	B−	Adopts a standardized attitude towards beliefs, behaviour, social attitudes and environment.

discrimination (as well as a valid coverage of the pupils' work) it is essential that assessments are made on a large number of occasions.

If it is necessary to mark the oral on a single occasion only, we would still recommend that a small mark scale is used. There must be serious doubts about anyone's ability to carry, for example, a scale of 30 marks in his head so that he can apply it consistently to all pupils. With the difficulties already referred to in connection with the conduct of the oral, it hardly seems likely that anyone could simultaneously detect fine differences such as are implied by a 30-point scale *and* record these reliably in the form of marks. It is not suggested that there would be any difficulty in consistently distinguishing a child in the 25+ mark range from one scoring less than 10; what is in question is whether marks of 25, 26, 27 (or 8, 9 and 10) do in fact represent differences of attainment, or whether they are more a reflection of the marker's variability. It seems likely that, in such cases, the 30-mark scale is doing no more than giving the appearance of greater accuracy than is capable of being achieved in practice.

Where it is necessary, therefore, to allocate more than a small percentage to the oral, we would recommend that the operational marking is done on a scale of not more than 10 marks, with subsequent multiplication of the scores to achieve the desired weighting, thus:

$$\text{(oral mark out of 10)} \times 3 = \text{final mark out of 30}$$

However, if even moderately large numbers of children are involved, this may result in inadequate discrimination; in such a case we would suggest that the oral marks are divided either **a** with a separate mark allocation for different aspects of the whole performance, or **b** with a separate mark allocation for each of several sub-tests into which the whole test is broken down.

As an example of **a**, a test of reading aloud in French might be marked as follows:

i	accuracy of pronunciation of individual sounds	5
ii	phrasing and grouping	5
iii	intonation and fluency	5
iv	understanding	5
	Total:	20

It must be said, though, that it is not easy to separate, from the impression of the reading as a whole, assessments under these separate categories (and, of course, the categories themselves might be disputed). A common practice, which is some help, is to make a cross on the mark sheet, or on the teacher's copy of the reading passage, when an error is noted in one of the more straightforward areas such as accuracy of pronunciation; a tick can be marked for particularly good pronunciation of a difficult word, for example, or for lively intonation of perhaps

86

a piece of dialogue in the passage. This allows for some objectivity in the marking. It is not, however, just a matter of adding the ticks and subtracting the crosses – they are no more than a guide, and must be supplemented by an overall impression, particularly in aspects such as fluency and understanding.

An alternative method, which is worth experimenting with, is to mark, say, the first three sentences for pronunciation only, and by specifying on the mark sheet perhaps five particular words which are to be marked, these can be marked 1, $\frac{1}{2}$ or 0. In the next sentence, marks may be awarded only for grouping of words into phrases; in the next, intonation only, and so on. Marking will certainly be more accurate, but the method relies on taking only a small sample of each aspect of the reading, hence its validity may suffer. On the other hand, if the reliability of impression marks on the whole passage is in doubt, then this must affect the validity of the other method also.

In some ways, therefore, there are advantages in the sort of division suggested under **b** above. For example, an oral test on ordnance survey map work with junior forms might be split into sub-tests as follows:

i   understanding of symbols and conventions   5
    (5 questions, marked 1, $\frac{1}{2}$ or 0)
ii identification of prominent features, from photographs, field sketches
    or models 10
iii ability to understand grid references   5
iv appreciation of topographical features and relationship to:
    (*a*) centres of population   5
    (*b*) communications   5
                                                    Total: 30

It would, of course, be possible to test many (or even all) of these aspects of map work in a written paper, and undoubtedly subject specialists will be able to suggest refinements which would make better use of oral techniques. The example is intended as an illustration only, but we would mention again the very real risk that a written examination may underrate the attainment of children who have difficulty in expressing themselves in writing. The oral test also has considerable advantages in its flexibility – for example, to accommodate the divergent thinker in a way that the more formalized written examination may not be able to do.

Much more work needs to be done on oral examining but we are convinced that there are great possibilities in this area.

Aural (listening) tests

Closely related to the oral are aural tests, at present widely used only in modern languages. Linguists distinguish between the *productive* skill of expression in the foreign language and the *receptive* skill of understanding; in the conventional oral test, with question and answer, both skills are involved. If it is possible to isolate those parts of the oral which are purely receptive, and to test these separately, then at the same time the validity of the whole scheme of examination will be improved (because we can come nearer to the ideal of testing one thing at a time) and the oral itself can be refined (and possibly shortened) by concentrating more exclusively on productive skills.

The great advantage of the aural test is that it can be done on a group basis, even with a whole class, if acoustic conditions are reasonably good, thus making administration of the test much less of a problem than with the oral. Standardized conditions can easily be achieved by using a tape-recording though, given agreement among colleagues in a school about matters like the speed of reading etc., it can be satisfactory to have the test material read out by the teacher.

It is perhaps misleading to have used the words 'read out' in the preceding sentence, because of its implications of reading aloud from a textbook. Not many people actually speak like a textbook and it is a misuse of aural techniques if the material consists of no more than a written passage spoken aloud. Differences between the spoken and written languages are much greater than are sometimes realized and the difficulties experienced by some children in understanding the textbook may in part be due to their unfamiliarity with written styles as well as to deficiencies in reading skills.

It has been a serious shortcoming in many aural tests in modern languages, as well as in the few aural tests that have been set in English, that they have tested the aural perception of passages which were intended to be perceived visually. It must surely be making less than full use of the aural test as a test of comprehension of language, in the widest sense, if no advantage is taken of the opportunity to use different voices, to test understanding of tone and intonation, of the relationship between the characters in a dialogue and of changes in attitude as the piece progresses. In addition, the spoken language contains redundancies, repetitions, fillers, such as 'you know', which are absent from the written form but which perform a vital function in speech since they allow the speaker time to compose the next sentence and the listener time to process the information. We would refer readers to the Schools Council Research Study, *The Quality of Listening* (Macmillan Education, 1974) by Andrew Wilkinson and his colleagues. This contains an extremely interesting analysis of the distinctive features of the spoken language and of the abilities required of the listener.

In the paragraphs above, we have been discussing the aural test as a test of proficiency in language; we would consider that there could also be a place for aural tests in other subjects as a supplement to the oral, though it must be recognized that this is relatively untrodden ground, except in so far as informal classroom tests are sometimes read out by the teacher. It would seem likely that, where standard set questions are to be used as part of the oral, it may be possible to administer at least some of these on a group basis in the form of an aural test with written answers; for example, some parts of the map-reading test on p. 87 could be treated in this way. It is appreciated that there are objections to 'contaminating' an aural test by asking for written answers and it would be advisable to arrange the questions so that only a word or two, a numeral, or even a tick or a cross is necessary to answer.

Of course, the example we have given is still doing no more than test through the medium of speech what could, for children unhampered by reading difficulties, be tested in a written paper. In certain subjects, however, there may well be cases (as suggested in Chapter III, p. 64) where aural comprehension could be worth testing in its own right and where material which is intended to be perceived aurally is easily available. A radio weather forecast could be an example or it may be felt that the ability to understand and make use of information from a lecture or a broadcast talk is important – certainly there seems to be quite widespread use of BBC schools radio and also a growing amount of taped material available in many subjects, which indicates an increasing reliance on aural techniques of instruction by many teachers. In some subjects, too, the aural understanding of specialized vocabulary might be important, or the ability to comprehend verbal instructions. What we are saying, in effect, is that there is a movement among many teachers away from reliance on the textbook as the main teaching medium towards a more comprehensive battery of techniques – aural, visual, audiovisual, as well as the written word. As yet, our testing methods have not really reflected this change.

There are two factors peculiar to aural testing which must be mentioned. The first is the effect of memory: a child may have understood a particular point at the time of hearing it but, possibly becoming confused by later material, has forgotten the answer when the time comes to write it down. For this reason, it is common in languages to arrange for several repetitions of the material and often to allow notes to be made. Even if a continuous piece is used, it may be broken into three or so sections with a few questions after each. Alternatively (or sometimes in addition) the children are given the questions before the test starts so that they can listen purposefully, with some idea of the information which is being sought – a situation which is reasonably parallel to a real-life situation, when one usually has some prior knowledge of the topic and what one is listening for.

Related to this is the second factor: the child has no control over the material he is being presented with – he cannot go back over the difficult bits and he must deal with the information as it comes, in a continuous sequence. For this reason, it is not advisable to set an aural test at too high a level, nor to arrange it so that the later part is considerably more difficult than the earlier, or the weaker pupils will have to sit uncomprehending, without the facility for checking over what they have been able to do, or puzzling out the harder parts. If it is necessary to include sections to discriminate among the more able pupils, it is better to distribute them throughout the test, so that a hard question is followed by an easier one and all the children can keep going.

Practicals

Like the oral, practical tests are difficult and time-consuming to organize and their reliability has been criticized.*

For these reasons, a practical test should not be undertaken lightly; as always, it is necessary to be quite clear about the precise nature of practical ability in relation to each subject. For example, the ability to make models in history or geography may be very useful and may provide the teacher with valuable aids to use in his lessons; nevertheless, one may be a perfectly competent historian or geographer without possessing this skill. In relation to these subjects, therefore, it would probably not be thought proper to make an assessment of practical ability as such. While model making may be a desirable activity to encourage in the classroom, if it is only a means of acquiring historical or geographical understanding, the important thing from the teaching/learning point of view would be how much of this understanding has in fact been acquired; it is, then, the degree of understanding which should be assessed, not the degree of skill in modelling.

It is important, too, to distinguish between *product* and *process*; different methods will have to be adopted depending on whether it is the finished article which is important or whether it is the method of working, the degree of manual dexterity in handling equipment, etc. which must be observed.

The old-style science practical, consisting of perhaps one or two experiments to be carried out in three hours or so, has been justifiably criticized on the grounds of poor validity and reliability; since the actual assessment was usually made on the pupil's written record of the experiment only, there must be considerable doubt about just what was being assessed. It is possible to imagine a case where the experiment had been correctly carried out but where a mistake in recording led to a very low mark being awarded. Conversely, one can conceive a situation where a pupil, knowing the results which would be expected, might claim to have achieved them, despite his lack of expertise in handling the apparatus. These are, of course, extreme examples which are intended only to illustrate some of the problems which may arise and to underline the point that if the *process* is important, then the assessment should not be made solely on the finished article – whether, as in this case, it is the report of the experiment, or

* For example, in science, see Philip E. Vernon's *The Measurement of Abilities* (University of London Press, 1972), p. 243.

whether it is a piece of metalwork, etc. This implies that, in some cases, the only way in which pupils can be assessed is by direct observation as they work; it need not always be so, however – the way in which the joints in a piece of furniture were made can be seen later if the joints are left unglued or the stitching of seams in a dress can be inspected if the lining is not sewn in.

The validity of a practical test can be improved if an examination of the station type is arranged. By organizing a series of comparatively short sub-tests, a number of experimental situations are provided and each child moves from one to another in turn. This allows for better syllabus sampling than one long test can achieve and, by careful arrangement of the sub-tests, a variety of skills can be tested. The station-type practical requires careful planning if best use is to be made of the time and laboratory or workshop space which it takes.

As an illustration, part of an experimental station-type practical in home economics is given below;* the whole practical examination is intended to last several hours (though divided into two parts) and would obviously present formidable problems of organization and resources for most schools. Three tests only are given here; the rest of the examination included the preparation of a simple meal, testing the hardness of water, removing stains from clothing, identifying cuts of meat, etc.

TEST A (Time allowed 30 minutes)

Material provided: meal for one, consisting of scotch eggs, tomato, roll and butter, fruit salad
Task:

(a) Make a time plan to show how you would set about preparing this meal.
(b) What is the approximate cost of the meal?
(c) Of what value is this food to the body?

TEST B (Time allowed 10 minutes)

Material provided: cake in which fruit has sunk, pastry which has shrunk in cooking, scones which are flat, a crinkled piece of nylon, a piece of table-linen ironed too dry
Task:

Look at these five examples and state *what* is wrong with them and *why* it has happened. (1) Cake (2) pastry (3) scones (4) nylon (5) table-linen

* Adapted from Schools Council Examinations Bulletin No. 9, *The Certificate of Secondary Education: Trial Examinations: Home Economics* (HMSO, 1966), pp. 40–2.

91

TEST C (Time allowed 15 minutes)*

Material provided: short length of 2-cord flex, short length of 3-cord flex, 13 amp ring circuit plug or 15 amp ordinary plug (depending on what is used in locality), a small screwdriver of the correct size, penknife or pliers
Task:

Connect the most suitable flex for an electric iron to the plug provided. State what kind of flex was used.

In view of the organizational problems of a full-scale examination of this nature, it is necessary to consider what can be done to streamline the operation. As we said at the beginning of this section, it is essential to be clear about the nature of the practical work. Test A depends on the written answer and might well be tested equally effectively in a theory paper. Test B, on the other hand, requires the presence of actual samples of scones, table-linen, etc. if the children are to identify what has gone wrong. Test C is again of a different nature in that the pupils are asked actually to wire up the plug.

It is possible from these examples to identify three aspects which are being tested:

i *Knowledge* (Test A), which can be tested in a written or oral examination. In other practical subjects, knowledge, say of the properties of different timbers and their suitability for various purposes, could be tested in this way; or knowledge of the qualities of different materials for a dress or a blouse.

ii *Identification* (Test B), which requires actual examples (or possibly photographs or diagrams) but which may be tested on a group basis. Instances in other subjects might include identification of the different timbers or of the different materials referred to above, identification of appropriate tools or of various musical instruments, etc.

iii *Performance* (Test C), which must be tested individually, by each child carrying out the required task, e.g. actually connecting the flex to the plug, making a mortise and tenon joint or sewing a seam, rather than being asked to say how it is done and perhaps lacking the ability to do it.

Depending on the subject, of course, it may not be necessary to assess separately the three aspects that we have identified above; in art, for example, knowledge of the properties of different paints, of the techniques of using brush and palette knife, of the possibilities of different textures of canvas, etc. may be useful

* The different times allowed for the various tests will be noted. The potential build up of pupils at certain points can be avoided by providing materials for several examples of the longer tests and/or by arranging a planned rotation (the method adopted in the experiment), e.g. candidate 3 follow this order: stations 4, 5, 1, 3, 2.

to the pupil, but many teachers would say that it was the end-product that was important, not the means of reaching that end.

Obviously, there are considerable differences between subjects; all that we are saying is that, on grounds of expediency alone, it is advisable to eliminate from the practical test any aspect which can validly be tested by another means, and to restrict the practical to testing performance. If performance is the only aim of the teacher, then the practical is the only test; thus, the art teacher who was concerned only with this aspect would see no place for a written paper – for him, it would be absurd to ask children to write (or to talk) about how they would paint a picture, rather than getting on and doing it. Another teacher, however, might have a place in his teaching for critical appreciation or for a knowledge of the history of art, in which case written or oral tests would be appropriate as well as the practical.

Concentrating on the practical as a test of performance in the sense in which we have defined it, organizational difficulties may be lessened by continuous assessment, or, a better term, by 'intermittent' assessment during the course. Thus, taking the variety of tasks set in the station type of practical, it may be possible to arrange them so that they are done at intervals throughout the term rather than all at once. However, it must be pointed out that, unless all the children can do each sub-test simultaneously, there may be problems of security; also that there may be similar drawbacks to those mentioned in connection with the oral with regard to the continuing development of children's abilities and the variation of attainment from the beginning of the term to the end.

It is apparent, also, that in most practical subjects the three aspects that we have identified above form a hierarchy and that effective performance must be based upon adequate knowledge and the ability to identify materials, equipment, etc. A similar but more detailed specification (in relation to science subjects) is suggested by Whittaker in his contribution on the assessment of practical work in *Techniques and Problems of Assessment* (ed. H. G. Macintosh); the specification can be summarized as:

a knowledge of apparatus
b knowledge of procedures
c knowledge of ways of using apparatus
d the ability to use apparatus
e the ability to implement procedures
f the ability to select appropriate procedures for a particular practical problem
g the ability to observe the material under investigation
h the ability to observe changes or differences taking place in the material under investigation

i the ability to record appropriately observed material and the changes which take place in it

j the ability to devise new apparatus or techniques to meet the demands of a particular problem

k the ability to plan and carry out a practical investigation

l attitudes to practical work.

With the exception of l, it will be seen that the abilities are listed in ascending order of complexity and that the pupil who possesses ability k must have passed through all the previous stages.

The implication of the preceding remarks is that at an advanced level of work it may become unnecessary to set a practical or to test separately the different aspects of practical ability in any given subject. The course work is also the work to be assessed, or, to put it another way, the test lasts the whole way through the course. The entire term, for example, may be spent by a pupil on an extensive project such as the construction of a substantial piece of furniture or the designing and making of an outfit of clothes. All the basic knowledge and more elementary skills which the pupils have acquired in the earlier stages of the course have now to be applied to the successful completion of a major task. In such cases, the organizational problems of the practical test are virtually eliminated and the assessment will be a mixture of what is much more genuinely continuous assessment (a constant updating of the teacher's judgement as the work proceeds) and a final evaluation of the end-product.

Assessment of practical work

As with the oral, the difficulties of practical assessment are much reduced where there is a permanent end-product, which can be considered at leisure. Where the assessment has to be made on the spot, either because it is a process which is being observed or because the end-product is perishable or transient in nature, the problems are severe.

We would suggest similar strategies to those recommended for the oral, i.e. a very short mark scale, clear identification of the various aspects of the work which are to be assessed, assessment on a number of occasions and/or separation of the whole test into several shorter sub-tests.

For example, in a trial scheme for the assessment of practical work in chemistry at A level,* the following abilities and attitudes were identified:

A Manipulative skills

B Skill in observation and the accurate recording of observations

* Trial scheme for University of London (Syllabus B) GCE A-level chemistry. Quoted in Schools Council Examinations Bulletin 27, *Assessment of Attainment in Sixth-form Science* (Evans/Methuen Educational, 1973), pp. 66–70.

C   Ability to interpret observations
D   Ability to devise and plan experiments
E   Attitudes (e.g. persistence, resourcefulness, enthusiasm, etc.).

Teachers in the trial scheme were asked to make assessments of abilities A–D on at least three occasions, bearing in mind that any one experiment might offer particular scope for assessing only one or two aspects, and to cover the whole range of chemistry, not concentrating only on a few areas. Each ability was to be assessed on a five-point scale according to the scheme:

5 – Outstanding
4 – Good
3 – Average (in relation to A-level candidates)
2 – Weak
1 – Poor.

A global assessment of attitude was to be made on the same scale at the end of the term or alternatively at the end of the course.

Where appropriate, a checklist makes it easier to achieve an objective assessment. Still with chemistry, here is an example * of a question in a practical test which is aimed at testing observation and deduction:

[The examiner gives instructions to the candidate in the following terms.] I am going to heat the contents of this test-tube and I want you to assume that you are describing the changes to a person who cannot see the test-tube. This means that you will have to tell me everything that you see happening, no matter how trivial or obvious it may seem.

[The examiner heats chromium (III) nitrate and, as the candidate describes the changes that occur, his observations are checked off on the following list.]

Mark sheet
Melting (or solution)   ......
Steam (or gas)   ......
Goes dark green   ......
Black residue   ......
Brown gas   ......
Splint rekindled   ......

[The examiner holds a glowing splint in the gas being emitted.]
[The examiner then asks 'What is the gas?' and depending on the answer

* Adapted from Schools Council Examinations Bulletin 21, *CSE: an Experiment in the Oral Examining of Chemistry* (Evans/Methuen Educational, 1971), pp. 64–5.

given – oxygen or nitrogen dioxide – takes one of the two routes to the end of the question.]

Route 1 (O_2)
What colour is oxygen?   ......

Route 2 (NO_2)
How do you know it is nitrogen dioxide?   ......

What is the other gas?   ......
Is anything else given off?   ......

What type of substance was heated?   ....

Which of these do you think it might have been?   ....

[The examiner shows a card with the names of five compounds on it: nitrate of potassium, of copper, of chromium, of sodium, of lead.]

By simply marking a tick or a cross in the appropriate space on the mark sheet, a detailed record of the candidate's responses can be made. The ticks and crosses on each pupil's assessment sheets for the whole test (composed of five sub-tests) can then be converted into a mark by applying the appropriate mark scheme, with the desired weighting for the different parts of each question.

A checklist can also be useful if it is desired to observe pupils when carrying out a process, each step of which can be identified and ticked off as completed. Similarly, observance of safety precautions in handling tools or hygiene in the preparation of food can be rapidly assessed in this way. A checklist for food hygiene, for example, might start in this way:

1   Ties back or covers long hair   ...✓...
2   Puts on clean protective clothing   ...✓...
3   Washes hands before handling food   ...✗...

Whatever method of assessment is adopted, there will be advantage, as always, if prior discussion can take place among members of a department about criteria for judgement and standards of marking. Also, if at all possible, trial assessments should be carried out and results compared and discussed. Although we have tried to suggest ways in which the assessment of practical work can be made more objective, it is clear that, in many subjects, some part (perhaps even a major part) of the assessment must depend on subjective judgements. It has been shown by experience in the field of public examinations that participation in trial markings and discussion among colleagues is the most effective way of achieving agreement about what constitutes good or bad work in a particular subject, and just how good (or bad) it is.

Projects

So far in the book, we have been looking mainly at methods of assessment which exist in their own right, that is, at the classroom test, the school examination, the oral and the practical, which are, by our earlier definition, situations set up specifically for the purpose of making an assessment. We have, inevitably, digressed at various stages to consider alternatives in the form of course-work assessment and in this section and the next, we shall consider in more detail the situation where the work is done for its own sake, irrespective of whether or not it is to be assessed.

Project work is undertaken in many subjects because of its value as a teaching/learning device, and this value would remain even if no assessment were made. Nevertheless, like any other piece of work, the project can be assessed and if a fair proportion of a child's time during the term, either in class or out of school, is spent on it, it may be felt that it ought to be.

The assessment must be based on the reasons for giving project work to the children, or, in other words, must be related to the skills and abilities which it is hoped will be developed by this sort of activity. A complication is, however, introduced by the fact that, for many teachers, an important aspect of the project is that it allows individual children to pursue a particular topic in which they have an interest; the implication of this is that the subject-matter of the project is unlikely to be common to all the children's work and comparisons between one project and another become more difficult.

It may be helpful to make separate assessments under various headings, such as:

Presentation (neatness, clarity, appropriate use of illustration, etc.)
Research (references, bibliography, personal investigations, etc.)
Content (coherence, relevance, continuity and significance)
Conclusions (interpretation of evidence presented).

These can be weighted as appropriate. It is almost certain, however, that content, and the conclusions drawn from the content, would be considered the most important aspects of the work and these, of course, are also the most difficult to assess, so the suggested method is of only limited usefulness.

To a certain extent, the assessment of the content is similar to assessing a long essay (see the considerations involved in essay marking in Chapter III, pp. 66–72). There are, however, some additional problems which must be mentioned, apart from the probably greater length of a project compared with an essay.

There is the old enemy, halo effect: because of the greater length it is more likely that poor handwriting or untidy presentation may erode one's standards of judgement on the content. Conversely, neat work (and girls often take much greater care over the appearance of their work than boys) becomes a pleasure to read and may receive a disproportionately high reward. Even if a separate mark allocation is given for presentation, it is not easy to be sure that one's assessment of content has not also been affected by tidiness or the lack of it.

Another way in which halo effect can work is through sheer bulk: a massive project, perhaps of 10 000 words, with copious references, illustrations, etc. may stun the marker into giving it a high grade, even though it may be a product more of blind persistence rather than of any real understanding. It may well be thought desirable to insist on a fairly tight limitation of length, say, not more than 3000 words, to discourage the 'over-kill' approach. It would probably be agreed in any case that a shorter project encourages children to develop selectivity in the material they use, to concentrate on the main issues and to exclude irrelevancies, while the weaker pupils will be less tempted to indulge in large amounts of copying from textbooks in order to achieve what seems to them to be an impressive length.

There is, indeed, evidence to suggest that a strict limitation of length and/or time improves the quality of the work considerably; it is essential also that the children, at any rate until they have considerable experience of this sort of work, are given careful guidance by the teacher on choice of subject and on method.

It seems reasonable, too, that if the teacher is quite clear in his own mind as to what qualities he looks for in a good project – in other words, about the criteria he will use for assessment – and if the children also are made aware of these criteria, they will produce better work.

It has been reported* that pupils produce the best individual studies in circumstances where:

a a manageable problem is defined;

b a hypothesis or generalization is advanced or model formulated;

c data are collected (by first-hand observation through field work or from other sources e.g. census returns) even if quite limited;

d data are analysed and presented (including the making of maps and diagrams and the use of statistical techniques where these are appropriate);

e conclusions are reached which enable the hypothesis, generalization or model to be evaluated.

These remarks refer particularly to geography but it can be seen that a similarly precise formulation in other subjects would do a lot to discourage children from tackling manifestly unsuitable topics such as The Second World War, Fashion

* See *Curriculum Design and Management in Geography: a Handbook for School Based Curriculum Renewal*, Schools Council Geography 14–18 Project, Teacher's Handbook (Macmillan Education, 1976).

through the Ages or The History of the Arsenal Football Club (with particular reference to the current season).

Some people would argue that, with projects, it is important to assess not so much what is in the finished work as what the pupil has got out of it, and would insist that the most important part of the assessment is an oral discussion with the teacher after the project has been completed. The argument is similar in many ways to the discussion of the role of model making (at the beginning of the section on practicals, p. 90) in that the project is considered as a means of acquiring certain skills or of developing understanding, and in the oral, the teacher is attempting to find out to what extent this has been achieved as a result of the work that each child has done. There is some debate on this matter – others would hold that such qualities must inevitably reveal themselves in a good project and can therefore be assessed from that evidence alone – but, because project work may be partly completed outside school, there is a risk that it may not always be the child's own work; an oral test will quickly reveal whether or not this is the case.

A sort of half-way house between the project and the practical is field work in geography and some other subjects. If the assessment is made as the work is carried out, it is very similar to the assessment of certain types of practical work discussed in the previous section; if the assessment is based on the field notebook, then it is more like assessing a project, though with the difference that the subject-matter may be largely common to the group of pupils who shared the same field trip. It may be thought desirable to assess both aspects, practical skills as the work is done and the record of field work, together with conclusions and interpretation of results, as shown in the notebook. Some, however, would hold the view discussed above, that field work is only a means of developing geographical understanding which can be tested and assessed by other means.

The particular role of project work, field work and indeed of practical work is a matter for subject specialists to decide in relation to their own speciality, their own school and the particular group of children concerned. We shall not discuss such questions here, but rather shall urge that the matter *is* carefully considered, because (and this is a theme which runs through the book) it is not possible to devise a satisfactory scheme of assessment for any subject, or any aspect of a subject, unless the aims and objectives of the teacher are clearly defined.

Course-work assessment

We have referred to the assessment of course work several times in the preceding chapters and, in view of the known shortcomings of tests and examinations, it is sometimes claimed that continuous assessment of course work is a way of overcoming some of these difficulties. As readers must have come to expect by now, there is no perfect answer to problems of assessment, and course-work assessment has its advantages and disadvantages like any other method.

There is, of course, no reason why course work should be continuously assessed; it is perfectly possible, for example in English, for pupils to compile folios of writing during the term for an assessment at the end of term. We have already defined continuous assessment as the updating of the teacher's evaluation of a piece of work as it proceeds towards completion. What is often referred to as continuous assessment is perhaps more accurately described as intermittent or periodic assessment, i.e. one made at intervals, more or less frequent, during the course.

Most teachers give a mark or grade for each piece of homework or classwork as it is completed and probably one of the commonest forms of intermittent assessment is based on these marks: they are sometimes totalled at the end of the term to give a term-work order (as distinct from the exam order) and may appear on the report in the form of a grade or a percentage mark. We must make it clear that we would regard this as a very dubious procedure indeed. It is commonly the case that teachers use marks for homework etc. as a reward or as a spur, in relation to the teacher's concept of the child's potential; thus work of mediocre quality from a child of low ability might nevertheless receive a high mark, say 9 out of 10, because it was well above his normal standard, while an equally mediocre piece of work from an able pupil might be given only 3 out of 10 as an indication that he could do a lot better and must wake himself up a bit. Some teachers, on the other hand, attempt to mark objectively, according to a fixed standard, irrespective of which child produces the work; probably most teachers are not entirely consistent, but use a mixture of both methods.

We are not claiming that either is a 'best' method; what we are saying is that they are incompatible, and that marks given according to conflicting criteria must not be added together without the virtual certainty of producing meaningless and misleading results.

If term marks are composed of a mixture of homework marks, classwork marks and marks from periodic tests, it is almost certain that they will have been given on different bases and should not be combined without some form of adjustment which may not be easy to make. It is therefore advisable to keep marks from different types of work in separate sections of the mark book so that it is immediately clear that they are reflections of different types of assessment.

Marks given in relation to each child's ability are essentially a measure of progress, not of attainment; this can be seen if we consider the (admittedly unlikely) case of a class of children who work throughout the term consistently to the best standard of which they are capable – they will all end up with 10 out of 10 on each occasion, and with 100 per cent at the end of the term. The term mark, therefore, would show that they have all made equally satisfactory progress, though the actual level of attainment would be very different. It may be that, in certain circumstances, marks or grades which show only progress may be sufficient; it would probably be agreed, however, that there are other occasions when an assessment of each child's attainment in more absolute terms becomes necessary, for example when transferring pupils from middle to upper school, perhaps, or when entries for external examinations are being decided.

It is in such situations that it becomes essential to make sure that uniform standards of marking are applied by all teachers in a department and, if comparisons have to be made between a child's attainment in different subjects, by all the departments in the school. Assessment based on course work must, in fact, be just as carefully planned as a programme of tests and examinations, and may well be even more difficult to organize. We have mentioned on several occasions the problems of ensuring common standards of marking among members of a department. These problems exist even when children from different classes have taken the same examination, but they are much greater when the different classes have worked with different teachers with inevitably different approaches and different emphases, even though they have been following broadly the same syllabus.

It is, therefore, advisable to draw up a clear specification of how and when the assessment is to be made, what sort of work is to be assessed, what qualities are to be looked for, etc., in much the same way as the specification grid is prepared for an examination. For purposes of comparing standards, it is wise to ensure that at least some pieces of work are common to all groups and the head of department might decide to mark all these himself or, at any rate, to make a careful check on marking standards. Exchanging sets of work from time to time among colleagues is also a useful way of achieving a common accord, and, if a test or examination is set as well, it can be used to adjust the course-work marks from different teachers so that they can be assimilated on to a common scale; techniques of doing this are dealt with in Chapter VI.

The question of what form the assessments are to be expressed in must also be faced. It is common enough to find that a five-point lettered scale A–E is used for course-work assessments rather than percentage marks and it is a simple enough matter to convert total marks or a series of grades into a final grade on any desired scale (see Chapter V).

However, it is also common to find that not all teachers, even within the same department, use the scale in the same way: some teachers give few grade As (or even none at all) on the grounds that A represents perfection, and some teachers are reluctant to use the lowest grade because of its demoralizing effect on the child who receives it. This matter has been referred to before (see Chapter III, pp. 68–9), but we must return to it here, though in a different context. The head of department will have available all the marks for all teaching groups and he can interpret B+ from the teacher who never gives higher than this as equivalent to another teacher's A. Similarly, the year tutor, or form teacher, looking at the range of grades in different subjects, can see that a B in English does not necessarily mean the same as a B in mathematics.

However, the child gets only his own grade in the various subjects and neither he nor his parents, reading the report, have sufficient information to be able to interpret the grades (or marks) in the way that the teacher can; the information given to parents and pupils is in fact often misleadingly presented.

Whatever mark or grade scale is decided upon must be applied uniformly, in fairness to the children, and the staff of a department or of the school as a whole should agree on how this is to be done, rather than leaving it to individual preferences. It may be found that using only three grades encourages teachers to use the full range, although the objection to damning with the lowest grade a child who may be working to the best of his limited ability still remains. To overcome this, we would suggest using a five-point scale, A–E, of which only grades A–D would normally be used to cover the full range of attainment within each subject, with grade E being kept as a 'punishment' grade for children who are thought to be deliberately under-achieving.

This suggested method would allow children of low ability, who are trying hard, to retain some self-respect by not receiving the lowest grade. However, in a streamed or setted school it will unfortunately be the case that there will be a lot of Ds in the lowest band. This is, of course, inevitable, being a reflection of why streaming or setting was adopted in the first place; it is to be hoped, however, that the school report would avoid placing too much emphasis solely on academic attainment and that reference could also be made to many other important aspects of the child's education where the picture may be a little brighter.

The remarks so far on course-work assessment may seem to be rather negative: we do not wish readers to be under the impression that the picture is one of unrelieved gloom. Neither, however, would we wish anyone to feel that course-work assessment is an easy way out; in many ways it is the most demanding type of assessment for the teacher to carry out well. Course-work assessment can, however, offer certain advantages over tests and examinations. In course-work assessment:

i   improved validity is possible since the whole of the syllabus is covered;
ii work is done under more normal conditions, in the classroom and out of school;
iii a wider range of skills and abilities can be assessed;
iv a sub-standard performance by a child on one occasion will not unduly affect his final assessment;
v   feedback to the teacher on children's progress is almost immediate.

102

To what extent these advantages offset the disadvantages, or to what extent course-work assessment should be used instead of, or in conjunction with, school examinations are very much matters for each school to decide.

Summary of Chapter IV

Both oral and practical tests are difficult to organize and are time-consuming. Careful planning is needed to ensure good validity and both types of test may be less reliable than written examinations. Where appropriate, group assessment can reduce some of the organizational problems, as can intermittent assessment during the term. There is scope for the development of oral and aural tests in subjects other than languages. Specification of the test and of criteria for assessment will improve the marking of both orals and practicals; similarly, with projects, a clear specification of the qualities which constitute a good project and guidance from the teacher in planning should improve the quality of the work as well as helping the assessment. Course-work assessment needs careful planning and is in many ways the most difficult to organize, particularly in a large school; however, it offers some significant advantages over assessment by means of examinations alone.

Questions on Chapter IV

(Outline answers are given in Appendix A.)

1 A school offers pupils in the fourth year the opportunity of taking a two-year course in Russian with the emphasis on the spoken language and leading to a Mode III examination with a heavy weighting attached to the oral. To lessen organizational difficulties, the teacher in charge proposes not to have an oral test at the end of the fifth year but to carry out an intermittent assessment during the course. What factors should he bear in mind when planning the assessment?

2 The practical test in an examination in home economics consists of the planning and preparation of a three-course meal for two people. Ingredients are provided and $2\frac{1}{2}$ hours are allowed for the whole test. Assessment is based equally on the pupil's preparation sheet (assessed by an external examiner) and the teacher's assessment of the prepared meal. Comment on this procedure.

3 A group of senior pupils taking a course in classical studies decide to undertake the production of a Greek play as their project. What factors should be considered with regard to the assessment of the project?

4 A school report gives a term grade (A–E) and an examination mark (percentage); in six subjects one child's grades and marks were:

Subject	Term grade	Examination mark
English	B+	65
Mathematics	D+	51
French	B	73
History	C+	60
Geography	B	58
Science	B	45

How should the parents interpret these results?

Assignments

1 Prepare a specification for an oral or practical test; state the abilities which are to be tested, outline the test materials needed and/or the structure of the test, and devise a marking scheme.
2 Consider the appropriateness (if any) of aural testing in your own subject. Are there any aspects of the subject in which aural comprehension is particularly important at any level?
3 Prepare a scheme for course-work assessment for one year-group in your subject. State the number and nature of the assessments which are to be made and outline the method(s) by which you would achieve equivalent standards of marking between different teachers.

Suggestions for further reading

Extremely useful articles on the topics which have been covered in this chapter will be found in B. Hudson's *Assessment Techniques* (Methuen Educational, Education Paperbacks, 1973) and H. G. Macintosh's *Techniques and Problems of Assessment* (Edward Arnold, 1974).

On oral testing
BURNISTON, CHRISTABEL. *Creative Oral Assessment*. Pergamon Press, 1968.
   (Contains useful advice on oral examining in English.)
DYSON, A. P. *Oral Examining in French*. Modern Language Association, 1972.
Schools Council. *The Certificate of Secondary Education: Trial Examinations – Oral English* (Examinations Bulletin No. 11). HMSO, 1966.
Schools Council. *CSE: an Experiment in the Oral Examining of Chemistry* (Examinations Bulletin 21). Evans/Methuen Educational, 1971.

WILKINSON, ANDREW, STRATTA, LESLIE, and DUDLEY, PETER. *The Quality of Listening* (Schools Council Research Studies). Macmillan Education, 1974.
(From the Schools Council Oracy Project (11–18) and essential reading for anyone wishing to understand the nature and importance of aural comprehension. A battery of standardized tests, with tapes, test manual, etc. intended for use in schools has also been produced by the project team.)

On examining practical subjects
The following Schools Council Examinations Bulletins:
8. *The Certificate of Secondary Education: Experimental Examinations – Science.* HMSO, 1965.
9. *The Certificate of Secondary Education: Trial Examinations: Home Economics.* HMSO, 1966.
10. *The Certificate of Secondary Education: Experimental Examinations: Music.* HMSO, 1966.
13. *The Certificate of Secondary Education: Trial Examinations: Handicraft.* HMSO, 1966.
14. *The Certificate of Secondary Education: Trial Examinations – Geography.* HMSO, 1966.
18. *The Certificate of Secondary Education: the Place of the Personal Topic – History.* HMSO, 1968.
19. *CSE: Practical Work in Science.* Evans/Methuen Educational, 1969.
27. *Assessment of Attainment in Sixth-form Science.* Evans/Methuen Educational, 1973.

EGGLESTON, J. F. and KERR, J. F. *Studies in Assessment.* English Universities Press, 1969.
(Deals with alternatives to the traditional examinations in history and physics.)

V. The meaning of marks

In this chapter we shall deal more fully with various topics that have already been touched upon in previous chapters: the significance of marks and their interpretation, together with some methods of analysis. Though some lists of marks, graphs and diagrams are involved, no more mathematical ability is assumed than most people use in everyday life.

The concept of the true score

We have said enough in the preceding chapters for readers to have realized (if, indeed, they were not already well enough aware of the fact) that any mark or grade is, at best, only a very rough indication of a level of attainment. Because some of the procedures which will be described in following sections may involve scaling or adjusting marks – a procedure which some people regard with a somewhat irrational distaste – it is necessary to introduce the notion of the 'true score', which is an important concept in test theory.

The true score is defined* as the average score a person would obtain if he were able to take a large number of similar tests or examinations in the same subject.

Since, in real life, it is not possible for anyone to take a large number of similar tests, it follows that on any one occasion, a child's actual work (the *observed score*), being affected by the sources of variability we have discussed already, will almost certainly not be the same as his true score; if he is lucky, and gets all the questions he has revised for the night before, and is on top form, the child may well get a higher mark than his ability really merits. And, conversely, if he gets the 'wrong' questions or has a bad cold, etc., he will have a lower mark than he deserves.

We can say, therefore, that the observed score is made up of two components: (i) the child's actual ability and attainment (which would be shown by his true score if we could get it), and (ii) the margin of error in our inevitably inaccurate measuring instruments, which may act in his favour or not. Thus we can establish a simple equation:

$$\text{observed score} = \text{true score} \pm \text{error score}$$

* See D. L. Nuttall and A. S. Willmott, *British Examinations: Techniques of Analysis* (National Foundation for Educational Research, Slough, 1972), pp. 26–7.

Since the error score has to be either added or subtracted, it might seem that, as with physical measurements, we could take a large number of readings and the error would be cancelled out. There is a certain amount of truth in this (which is one of the justifications for course-work assessment as opposed to a one-off examination) but it is not an exact parallel with the scientist taking the average of several readings.

Practical difficulties prevent us from ever getting very close to the ideal: it is not possible to set a number of similar examinations and, even if it were, the child would be likely to suffer from boredom and fatigue. If we try to counter this by spacing out the tests, then there is the effect of learning between one test and the next. If we try to make a continuous assessment of course work, we shall probably find that we have to use less precise methods (because of pressures of time) than we can adopt in an examination situation. So, whatever we do, we are not going to be able to achieve great precision in educational measurement, certainly nothing like the accuracy of physical measurements of weight, height, etc.; a closer analogy would be with the scientist trying to measure, with an elastic tape-measure, the length of a worm which is itself constantly expanding and contracting.

There are several other important differences between physical and educational measurement (besides the imprecision of our test instruments) which must be made clear at this point. The fact that we give marks on a numerical scale can be misleading, since it tends to make us imagine that the mark scale is similar to other scales of length, temperature, weight, etc. This is most definitely not the case.

First, there are no upper or lower limits to what is being measured – a score of 100 per cent does not (*cannot*) mean that an individual knows everything about the subject, nor does 0 per cent mean that nothing is known. It is true that there may be an absolute zero: a test in Kurdish, for example, given to someone who knows only English would certainly lead to a mark of 0, which would be a fair reflection of attainment. But 0 might also be scored by someone who knows a very little Kurdish but not enough to register a mark; since most educational tests will be given to children who have some acquaintance with the subject, a zero score means that the child's knowledge is outside the range of the test, not that his knowledge is nil.

Secondly, the mark scale is not uniform. We cannot say that a mark of 50 per cent is twice as good as one of 25 per cent. All we can say is that, on one occasion, the child who scored 50 per cent did rather better than the child with 25 per cent. How much better, we have no means of telling and it may not even be meaningful to try to do so. Nor can we say that 75 per cent is as much better than 50 per cent as 50 per cent is than 25 per cent: the teacher may mark more severely at the top end or there may be a dozen or more children with marks better than 75 per cent, while those getting 50 per cent and 25 per cent might be a couple of tail-enders a long way behind the rest of the group.

In fact, we cannot even be too sure that 80 per cent is better than 70 per cent; quite apart from the inaccuracy of the test, there may be other aspects of the subject where the tables would be turned.

The best that can be said is that the mark resulting from any of the assessment procedures that we have been describing is a first approximation. We should not attach too much importance to any single result, nor to small differences in marks, or places, though the results of several assessments may indicate a general trend in a child's progress.

It follows from these remarks that one should not become too attached to the original mark given – the 'raw score' – but that one should be prepared to adjust it in some way if the need arises.

Raw scores

The initial marks resulting from any assessment procedure are termed raw scores and may well need further treatment before they are ready for consumption. Left on their own, marks can behave in a peculiar way; consider, for example, the lists of marks given in Table 5a in two subjects for a group of ten children.

Table 5a Marks (out of 100) in subjects X and Y for 10 children

Pupil	Subject X	Subject Y	Total marks
A	65	35	100
B	63	41	104
C	62	48	110
D	61	52	113
E	58	65	123
F	56	70	126
G	55	76	131
H	54	81	135
I	52	87	139
J	50	95	145

It will be seen that the order in subject Y is the reverse of that in subject X; yet, when the two lists are totalled, the final order is the same as the order in subject Y – in other words, subject X *has had no influence in deciding the final order of pupils* and the same result would have been obtained if only marks on Y had been used and the other marks thrown away.

108

Obviously, this is unsatisfactory and needs to be corrected. Perhaps subject Y has been marked more leniently than subject X; if we add the marks in each column and divide by the number of pupils, we can obtain the average mark or *mean** (strictly speaking, it is the *arithmetic mean*) for subjects X and Y:

Total for subject X: 576; mean: 57·6
Total for subject Y: 650; mean: 65·0

The difference between the two means is 7·4, so it would appear that subject X has been more severely marked (or that the children are better at Y than at X). However, if we attempt to correct this by adding 7·4 to all the marks in subject X, it will be found that no change in the final order occurs (see Table 5b).

Table 5b   Adjusted marks in subject X combined with marks in subject Y

Pupil	Subject X (+7·4)	Subject Y	Total marks
A	72·4	35	107·4
B	70·4	41	111·4
C	69·4	48	117·4
D	68·4	52	120·4
E	65·4	65	130·4
F	63·4	70	133·4
G	62·4	76	138·4
H	61·4	81	142·4
I	59·4	87	146·4
J	57·4	95	152·4
Mean mark	65·0	65·0	

If readers experiment further with these marks, it will be seen that even adding 30 per cent (the difference between the top mark on X and the top mark on Y) to all the scores on X causes no change in the final order which, indeed, will also be unchanged if all the marks on X are doubled. It is not until the marks for subject X are trebled that they begin to have some influence on the final result. Obviously one cannot proceed by blindly doubling or trebling marks in the hope that something will happen; there must be a more rational basis for action.

When two or more sets of marks are combined, what is most important in

* As we have already seen, since the error component in the observed score can be either plus or minus, it follows that the pluses and minuses will tend to cancel one another out when we are talking about the average mark of a group. In terms of the equation this means that: mean observed score = mean true score, or in other words, we can say that mean scores are likely to be more reliable than individual marks.

deciding the effect each list will have on the final result is not the possible maximum mark that could be awarded nor the mean of the marks, but the *range of marks actually given in each subject*. Thus, in subject X, the marks given to the ten children ranged between 65 and 50 (a range of 15 marks), while in subject Y the difference between top and bottom was 60 marks. The more the marks are spread out, the greater will be their influence on the final total.

In considering the range of marks, however, it is not enough to look at just the upper and lower limits; account must also be taken of the spread of the intermediate values, since a single freak result at the top or bottom of the class can give the impression of a good spread while the rest are bunched together in the middle. Obviously the way the marks are distributed is very different in the following two lists:

List A: 95, 53, 52, 51, 50, 49, 48, 47, 46, 15
List B: 95, 80, 70, 60, 55, 50, 45, 40, 30, 15

Statisticians measure the spread of marks in terms of the *standard deviation* (SD or σ) which is calculated according to a formula* which takes into account the distance each mark is away from the mean (its deviation from the mean, or average, mark). The standard deviations for lists A and B above and for subjects X and Y (for marks see Table 5a) are as follows:

List A: 18·14
List B: 22·45
Subject X: 4·76
Subject Y: 19·29

(The higher the value of the SD, the greater the spread of marks.)

Working out a standard deviation is a fairly lengthy operation but there are ways of approximating to it which come reasonably close. One method is to calculate the *semi-intersextile range*.

The *sextile* means simply one-sixth of the pupils; in any list, there will be an upper and lower sextile. To calculate the semi-intersextile range one counts one-sixth of the pupils down from the top of the order and one-sixth of the pupils up from the bottom; the range of marks between these two points is the inter-sextile range, which is then halved to give the semi-intersextile range.

In the nature of things, of course, the upper and lower sextiles will hardly ever correspond to an actual pupil's mark. Taking the figures for subject X, with ten pupils, the sextile will be at $1\frac{2}{3}$ pupils (10 divided by 6). On our list, therefore,

* The texts on educational measurement or statistics cited at the end of the chapter give a full explanation of the formula for calculating standard deviation. The relationship between the standard deviation and the normal curve is described in Chapter VI, pp. 142–3.

the cut-off point must be at $\frac{2}{3}$ of the way down between the first and second pupils, i.e. at 63·66. Similarly, the lower sextile will come (working upwards) at $\frac{2}{3}$ of the marks between pupils J and I, which is 51·33. The difference between these is 12·33 and halving this gives 6·17.

Similarly, for subject Y the values are: upper sextile 89·66; lower sextile 39·00; range 50·66; semi-intersextile range 25·33.

These results are close enough to the value of the standard deviation for most practical purposes; with larger numbers of pupils and more closely grouped marks one should get a rather closer correspondence unless there is an abnormal distribution of scores.

The advantage of working with the sextiles, rather than looking simply at the top and bottom mark, is that they are less likely to be affected by occasional freak results at either end.

We have seen, so far, how the mean of a set of marks can be calculated and their spread estimated, and how the attempt to combine raw scores without taking these factors into consideration resulted in one set of marks having no effect at all on the final result. It is a common belief that to ensure two (or more) sets of marks carrying equal weight, all that is necessary is to scale them so that the means and standard deviations are equal. Recent research,* however, has shown that this is not always the case and that account must be taken of the degree of similarity between the orders, as shown by the correlation (see pp. 112–21).

To achieve precisely the desired weighting involves an exceedingly complex computer programme and the advice given in many of the standard texts to scale marks to the same mean and standard deviation before combining them must be interpreted with some caution. It has been shown, in fact, that in some cases scaling before adding marks together may actually make matters worse and the final result may be even further from reflecting the desired balance between the different subjects than was the case with raw totals. However, it is not possible to say whether this is likely to occur or not and in view of the complexity of the operation the best advice that can be given is: do not attempt to combine marks from different subjects.

Quite apart from the difficulties of ensuring equal weighting in a combined total mark, it is doubtful if there is much point in attempting to do so; in our two subjects, X and Y, the two orders were exact opposites, i.e. the child who was top on one was bottom on the other. The two subjects are clearly quite different in the demands they make on the children and adding their marks together is like adding four apples to six pears – this can only be done by calling them ten pieces of fruit and you no longer know what sort they are.

* See Schools Council Examinations Bulletin 28, *CSE: Two Research Studies* by Diana E. Fowles (Evans/Methuen Educational, 1974).

Combining marks from different subjects may similarly result in a loss of information. This can be seen if we add the rank orders on subjects X and Y (and the two rank orders must automatically have the same mean and standard deviation): everyone comes out the same with a total of 11.

Clearly, there is more value in retaining the two separate orders in the different subjects than in attempting to arrive at a meaningless total which obscures the children's individual strengths and weaknesses.

On the other hand, when it is a matter of combining marks from different assessments within the same subject, it may be reasonable to assume that the marks are measuring attainment in the same area and it can be justifiable to add them together on the grounds that the total represents the result of repeated measurements of the same ability and so will tend to be more reliable than a single mark. The ranges of the marks should be made equal before addition (see pp. 124–6). As has been shown, it is possible that this alone may not be enough to ensure the desired weighting; it is likely, however, that no very serious injustice will be done if precisely the intended balance between the various components within a subject is not achieved.

Where it is felt that different aspects of the same subject *are* quite distinct, then the remarks above in favour of retaining separate assessments will still apply. Methods of estimating the degree of similarity in mark lists are dealt with in the next section.

Similarities between mark lists – correlation

The degree of similarity between sets of marks is termed their *correlation*, which is expressed as a figure between +1·00 and −1·00 (the correlation coefficient or r).

A correlation of +1·00 represents complete agreement between the two orders; they are identical and one could be substituted for the other without making any difference. A correlation of −1·00, on the other hand, means they are complete opposites, good on one is bad on the other; subjects X and Y in Table 5a have a correlation of −1·00. A correlation of 0·00 signifies that the two lists are completely unrelated in their rankings of the children.

Because of the imprecise nature of mental measurement, we can never expect to get perfect correlations of +1·00 (or indeed, of −1·00). Anything over +0·9 would be regarded as very high, and correlations of the order of +0·7 would normally be accepted as showing a reasonable degree of similarity. Figure 3 illustrates the correlation between two sets of marks; the marks on test P are on the left-hand scale and those on test Q along the bottom. Each point on the graph shows the mark of one pupil on each of the two tests; thus, the point marked A shows that one pupil scored 14 marks on test P but 8 marks on test Q.

112

The correlation of these marks is, in fact, not very high (+0·46) which is shown by the way the points are scattered over the graph;* a perfect positive correlation (+1·00) would show all the points along the dotted line from the bottom left corner to the top right. A negative correlation (−1·00) would give points lying along the opposite diagonal.

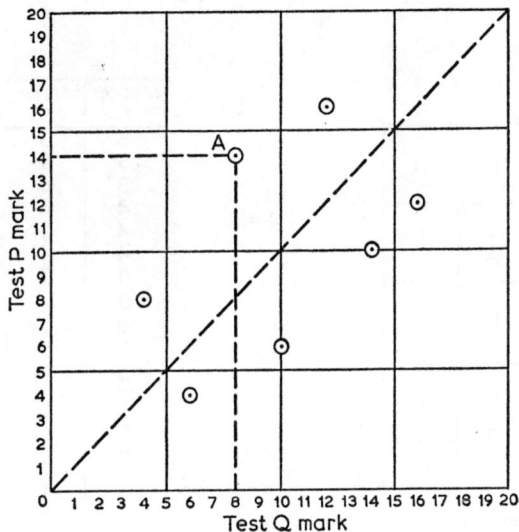

Fig. 3 Marks scored on 2 tests ($r = + 0·46$) by 7 pupils

The correlation between the marks given by two teachers to the same set of work will show, in similar fashion, the degree of accord between the markers. Again, +1·00 would show complete agreement but can never be attained except in marking an objective test. Figure 4 shows the results of two markers, R and S, marking 20 essays on a scale from 0 to 5.

In this case, because it is inevitable that more than one essay will be given the same mark, it is more convenient to arrange the graph so that each mark occupies a box on the squared sheet and a tally is placed in the appropriate place. Thus in the box marked B, two essays have been given 4 marks by both markers, while in C, marker R has given the essay only 2 marks, though S thinks it is worth 4.

The correlation between the markers in this case is fairly high (+0·79) showing that they are in reasonable agreement about the marking or that the *inter-marker correlation* is fairly good. In the same way, the correlation between one teacher's marks on a number of pieces of work and the marks he gives to the

* This type of graph is, appropriately enough, called a *scattergram*.

113

same work a month or two later would show his consistency as a marker; this is called a *mark–re–mark* correlation.

Correlations can also be worked out between results on mock examinations and the actual grades awarded, to give an indication of the predictive validity of the mocks, or between a test and another criterion (teachers' estimates, course-work assessments, etc.) to work out concurrent validity (see Chapter II, p. 29).

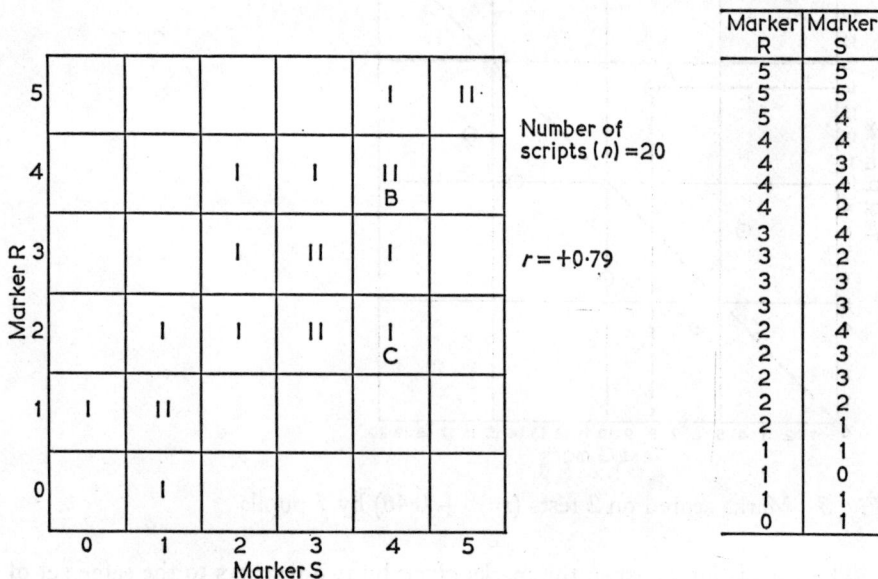

Marker R	Marker S
5	5
5	5
5	4
4	4
4	3
4	4
4	2
3	4
3	2
3	3
3	3
2	4
2	3
2	3
2	2
2	1
1	1
1	0
1	1
0	1

Number of scripts $(n) = 20$

$r = +0.79$

Fig. 4   Marks given by 2 markers for 20 essays on a scale 0–5

It must be remembered that a perfect correlation cannot be expected because there will be ineradicable sources of variability in both the marks and the criterion with which they are being compared. As can be seen from Figure 4, even when there is a reasonably high correlation, there can still be a certain amount of disagreement about individual cases. Further, sets of marks can show a high correlation even though the standards of marking are not in alignment. For example, when the order is similar but one set of marks range from 0 to 6 and the other from 6 to 10, there will still be a high positive correlation.

The correlation, therefore, shows at best only a rough sort of correspondence and results must, as always, be interpreted with caution.

114

Estimating the correlation coefficient – the HILO method

There are several formulae for working out the coefficient of correlation, all of which involve fairly lengthy calculations. Readers who are prepared to tackle these, or who have access to an electronic calculator or a computer, will find the formulae in any of the standard textbooks on educational measurement or statistics mentioned at the end of the chapter.*

For those who do not wish to undertake mathematical operations of such complexity, a method (devised by G. F. Peaker) of getting an approximation to the correlation coefficient can be used.

This procedure is called the HILO method and it is a simple way of getting a measure of the agreement between two sets of marks. Basically, it consists of dividing each list in half (a HIGH group and a LOW group); an individual child may then be HIGH on both lists, LOW on both, HIGH on the first and LOW on the second, or LOW on the first and HIGH on the second. The extent of the agreement is shown by the percentage who are in the HIGH–HIGH and LOW–LOW groups together (that is, the proportion about whom both mark lists agree). This percentage can be converted into a correlation coefficient, which we can call r_p, by reading off the value from a graph.

The method will be found quite straightforward to operate using the following steps:

1 *Plot the marks on a scattergram.* The scattergram should be drawn so that the marks occupy boxes (as in Figure 4), that is to say, the lines on the graph divide the marks from one another.† If a long mark range is being used, it may be convenient to group the marks into bands (23–25, 26–28, 29–31, etc.) as seems appropriate. Grouping marks causes a certain loss of accuracy, which is acceptable within limits for the sake of ease of working. As a rough guide, if it is found that more than 4 or 5 tallies (in a group of 25–30) occupy the same row or the same column, the mark groups should be made smaller (unless they are genuine ties, that is, pupils with the identical mark – if, for example, grades A–E are being used, it is inevitable there will be a lot of ties).

2 *On a piece of transparent paper or plastic, draw two lines at right angles to form a cross.* This is placed over the scattergram, which will be divided into four quadrants by the cross: the top right and bottom left quadrants will contain the HIGH–HIGH and LOW–LOW groups that we want to identify. The precise position of the cross is obviously important and it must be placed as near to the centre of the scattergram as possible; the aim will be to find the box which lies

---
* See also Appendix C.

† Ordinary squared paper will usually be found more convenient than graph paper.

in the centre of the array of tallies and then to place the cross at the diagonally opposite corners of this box (A and B) so as to get two readings:

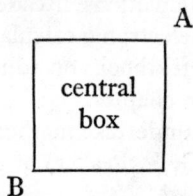

A

central
box

B

3 *To find the central box:*

i On the left-hand scale, find the line which divides the array so that there is an equal number of tallies above it and below. Then mark an arrow ($\rightarrow$) at the side, one space on the scale *above* this line. Similarly, mark another arrow, one space *below* the mid-line.

ii If there is an odd number in the group or if there are ties at the mid-point or if there is a gap in the middle of the range, it will not be possible to find a single line which divides the array in half. In this case, identify the *row which contains the mid-point(s)* (or the row where the gap occurs) and mark two arrows, one on the upper edge of this row and one on the lower.

iii Do the same on the lower scale. Mark two vertical arrows, each one space left and right of the vertical dividing line (if one can be found) or two vertical arrows marking the left and right edges of the column containing the mid-point(s), if there are ties, an odd number or a gap in the middle.

[*The central box is defined by the intersections of the four arrows.* Until one is used to the method, it will be helpful to mark in the position of the central box on the graph with a different coloured ink so that it stands out. The central box may contain one, two or four of the original mark boxes, depending on where the arrows are placed.]

4 *Place the cross over the scattergram so that the intersection falls on the top right-hand corner of the central box (point A).* Count the numbers of tallies in the top right-hand quadrant and in the bottom left-hand quadrant of the cross. *Then move the cross down to the opposite corner (B)* and again count the numbers of tallies in the top right and bottom left quadrants. The two readings may give the same total; if not, take the average.

5 *Multiply the result by 100 and divide by the total number in the group to express it as a percentage.* Values above 70 per cent begin to show a reasonable degree of agreement.

6 *Read off the value of r_p from the conversion graph* (see p. 119). This step is not essential; for comparative purposes within the school, it may be enough to use the percentage agreement resulting from step **5** above.

116

The method in use can be illustrated by means of the set of marks shown in Table 6. These are course-work and examination marks (both out of 100) for a class of 27 pupils. Figure 5 (p. 118) shows the marks arranged in groups of five (26–30, 31–5, etc.) for convenience and plotted on a scattergram. Having entered the tallies on the scattergram, as a check count the numbers in each row and mark the totals down the right-hand side; the same should be done for each column (totals at the top).

Table 6 Course-work and examination marks (out of 100) for 27 children ($n = 27$)

Course	Examination	Course	Examination	Course	Examination
42	22	45	43	49	40
81	47	65	60	47	18
76	33	44	54	68	59
88	66	69	55	41	42
51	37	85	74	68	68
64	32	35	18	60	53
39	40	50	49	66	56
79	58	87	73	27	26
80	66	89	84	57	49

With a group of 27 pupils, the mid-point should come at the 14th place (there are 13 higher and 13 lower). By counting down the left-hand scale, it can be seen that in fact the 13th and 14th places are tied, so we can mark an arrow above and below the mark group 61–5. Similarly, on the lower scale, there is a treble tie at 46–50 so arrows are marked to the left and right of this band.

The intersections of the four arrows define the central box (shown hatched). Placing the plastic cross first at position A (keeping the arms of the cross along the lines) and then at position B, it can be seen that the number of tallies at each position are:

2	10		2	12
12	3		9	4
Position A			Position B	

The totals for the top right and bottom left quadrants are:

Position A: $10 + 12 = 22$ Position B: $12 + 9 = 21$

Average of A and B: 21·5   Percentage: $\dfrac{21\cdot5 \times 100}{27} = 79\cdot6$

117

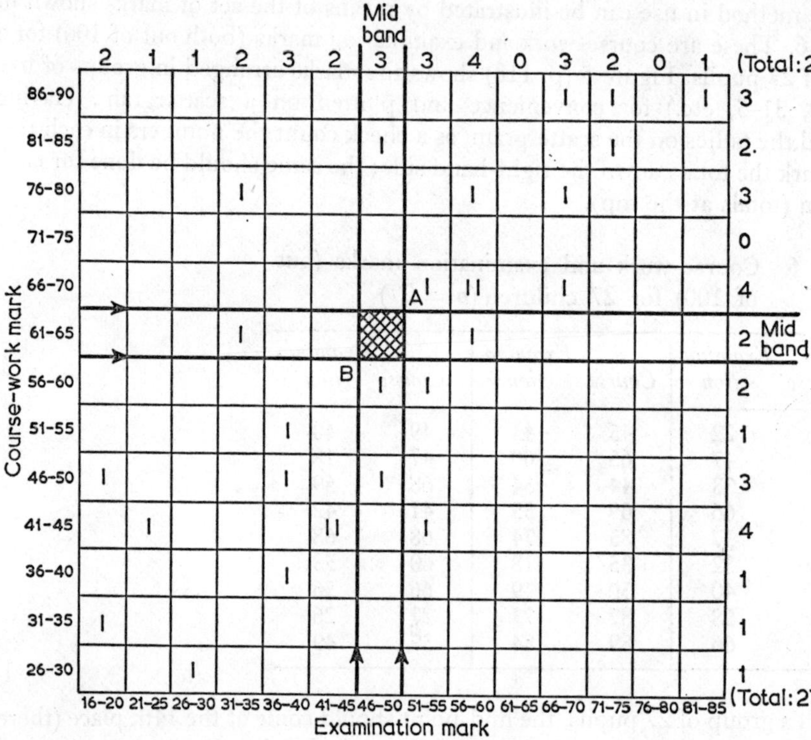

Mid band

2 1 1 2 3 2 3 3 4 0 3 2 0 1 (Total: 27)

Course-work mark (vertical axis) bands: 86-90, 81-85, 76-80, 71-75, 66-70, 61-65, 56-60, 51-55, 46-50, 41-45, 36-40, 31-35, 26-30

Row totals (right-hand column): 3, 2, 3, 0, 4, 2 (Mid band), 2, 1, 3, 4, 1, 1, 1 (Total: 27)

Examination mark (horizontal axis): 16-20 21-25 26-30 31-35 36-40 41-45 46-50 51-55 56-60 61-65 66-70 71-75 76-80 81-85 (Total: 27)

Fig. 5 Scattergram of course-work and examination marks (out of 100) for 27 pupils ($n = 27$)

For a percentage of 79·6, reading from the HILO percentage conversion graph (Figure 6), a value of r_p of 0·80 is obtained. By direct calculation, the correlation between the two sets of marks is 0·76. It must be noted that with numbers as low as 27, the formulae for direct calculation of r are not very reliable, since they can be heavily influenced by one or two freak results. In fact, a statistical test can be used to show that, with this example, the likelihood is that the true value of r lies somewhere in the range 0·54–0·88. It would seem that the HILO method is likely to give results which are usually within the margin of error of the direct calculation.

In the second example (see Figure 7), course-work grades, A–E, are being compared with test results (out of 15) for a group of 24 pupils. In this case, the C band contains the mid-point on the left-hand scale, but the lower scale can be divided in half exactly between marks 9 and 10. The central box is then identi-

118

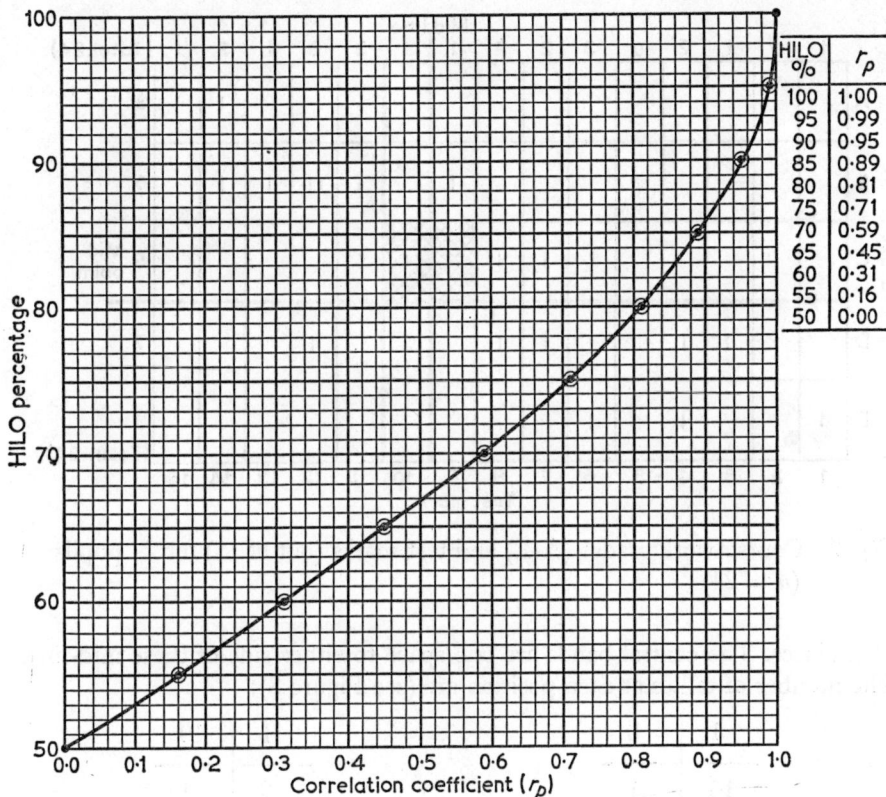

Fig. 6 HILO percentage/r_p conversion graph

fied by taking one space left and right of this vertical division. The number of tallies at each position are:

1	8		3	11
13	2		8	2
Position A			Position B	

The average reading is 20, or 83·3 per cent which gives r_p as 0·86. The direct calculation gives a value of r of 0·80.

The same method can also be used with rank orders rather than marks as is shown in Figure 8, where positions for a group of 20 pupils on two lists are plotted. In this case, we can divide both orders exactly between the 10th and

119

Mid line

1 0 1 2 0 3 2 2 1 | 2 3 3 1 2 1 (Total: 24)

Grade — A, B, C (Mid point), D, E

Test mark: 1 2 3 4 5 6 7 8 9 10 11 12 13 14 15

(Total: 24)

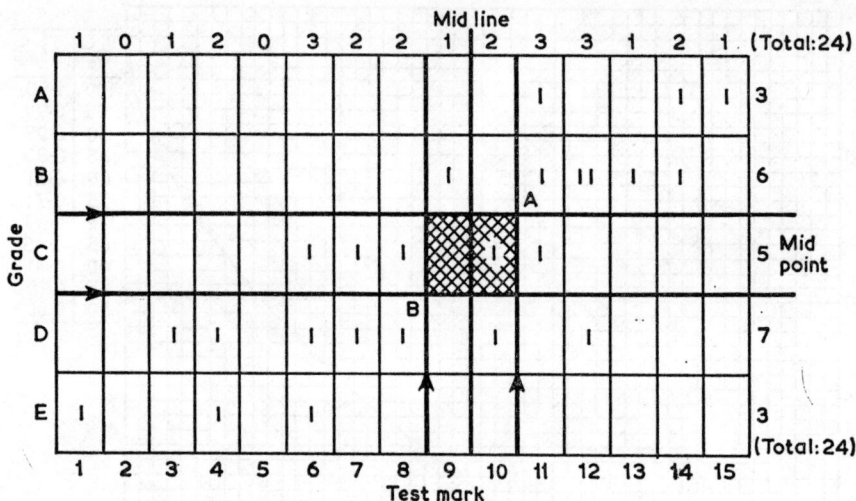

Fig. 7 Course-work grades (A–E) and test marks (out of 15) for 24 pupils
($n = 24$)

11th places. The central bands are one space to either side of these mid-lines.
The number of tallies at each position are (see Figure 8):

	1	8
	10	1

Position A

	1	10
	8	1

Position B

This gives a percentage of 90 and an r_p of 0·95. By direct calculation r is 0·93.

If larger numbers (a whole year-group for example) are involved, it is likely
that it will not be necessary to take two readings and it will probably be enough
just to write out one list as a rank order, and to write the corresponding place on
the second test beside it. Then the mid-point (divide ties in half, count the odd
one in the middle as HIGH) is picked out, and the HIGH–HIGHs and LOW–LOWs
are counted by going down the list. The procedure is then as described above.

It should be noted that any HILO percentage of less than 50 means a *negative*
correlation. If the percentage value found is subtracted from 100, Figure 6 can
be used to find the value of r_p with a minus sign added to it. Thus, if the HILO
percentage is 40, this is subtracted from 100 (60 per cent). The value of r_p for
60 per cent is 0·31 and since 40 per cent means a negative correlation, r_p is
−0·31.

The HILO method is an approximation but it will give an idea of the size of

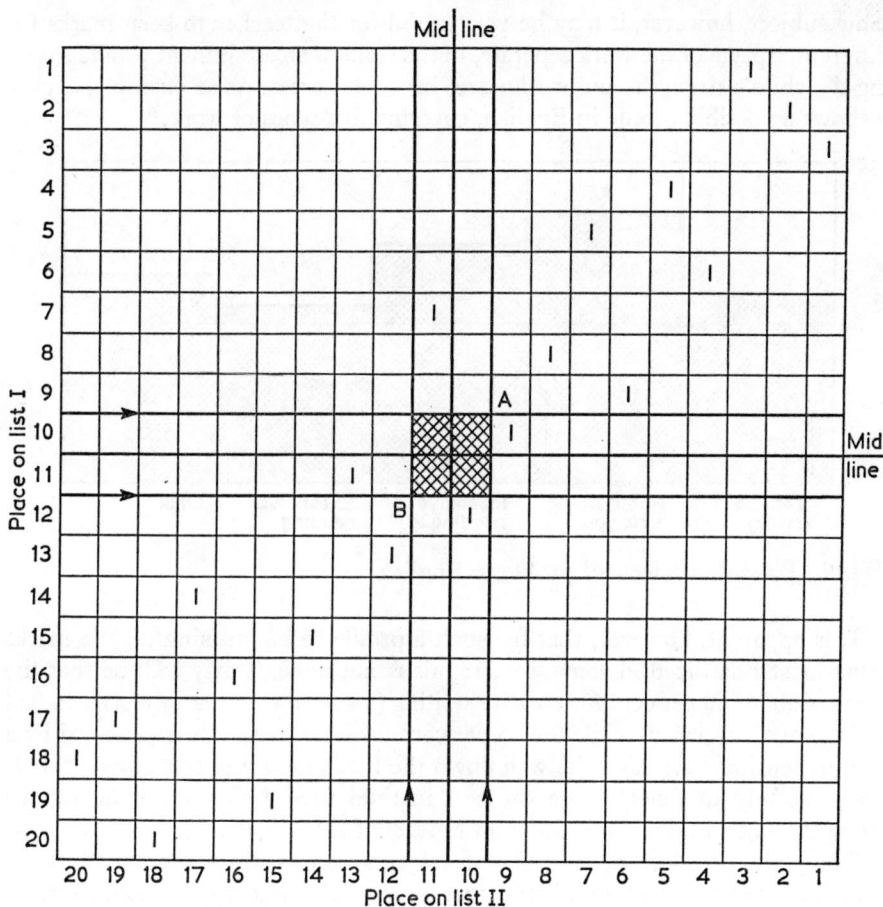

Fig. 8 Rank orders on 2 mark lists for 20 pupils ($n = 20$)

correlation that exists; in most cases, it will be within 0·1 of the directly calculated value, though it must be remembered that as the value of r approaches 0·00, results of the direct calculation with small numbers become much less reliable. For our purposes, however, we can say that a HILO percentage of around 75 per cent ($r_p = 0·71$) or better indicates an acceptable degree of correlation.

Standardizing marks

At the beginning of this chapter we showed how combining marks from different subjects could lead to a loss of information about the children; even within the same subject, however, it may be very useful for the teacher to keep marks for different aspects of the work separate, in the form of an attainment profile showing the child's strengths and weaknesses in various areas. As an example, Figure 9 shows a possible profile in English, covering five types of work.*

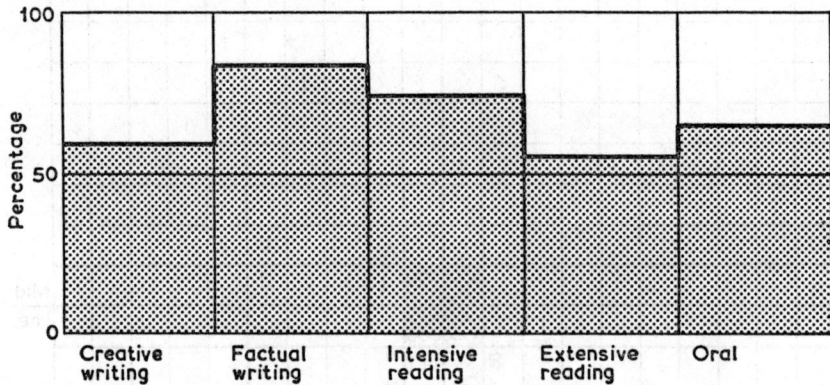

Fig. 9 Possible attainment profile in English

It is apparent, however, that for such a profile to be meaningful, the marks must be standardized in some way. If this is not done, it may well be that the mark of about 60 per cent for creative writing (assessed by an essay test) is in fact the top mark awarded, while the 75 per cent for intensive reading (assessed by a comprehension test) might be well down the list. The use of raw scores, therefore, is likely to reflect more the test method used rather than the pupil's strengths and weaknesses in different aspects of the subject.

The child's attainment in different subjects also provides a profile and the same arguments for standardizing marks or grades also apply. Some sort of comparability of marking must be established if meaningful comparisons are to be made between different areas of the curriculum. Some simple methods for standardizing marks and grades are outlined below.

Using rank orders or percentiles

Expressing results in terms of rank order, or as percentiles, within the class, or within the year-group, eliminates differences in marking standards. Rank orders also ignore the differentials between pupils, which some teachers may wish to show in terms of marks. For example, a child who is given a mark of 95 per cent, with the next highest mark 70 per cent, is a long way ahead of the rest of the

* This is intended to illustrate a point only; subject specialists will undoubtedly be able to work out an improved version in English and in other subjects.

122

group, although in terms of rank order the difference is only one place. This drawback is minimized as the size of the group increases; it is less likely that such a gap in the ability range will exist in a complete year-group in a large school. Problems can arise where groups are split for certain subjects, or where it is necessary to compare rank orders between teaching groups of different size. For example, is the child who is tenth in a class of 27 children doing as well as a child who is eighth in a parallel form of 25?

Turning the rank order into a percentile overcomes some of these problems. Using percentiles simply means that the child's position in a group of 25 (or whatever size it is) is converted into what the position would be in a class of 100. This is done for the same reason that marks out of a working total of 80 or 120 are converted into percentages – to enable comparisons to be made on a similar basis.

Like percentages, percentiles range from 100 downwards. If a child is on the 90th percentile in a group, it means he is as good as or better than 90 per cent of the children in that group; the 50th percentile represents an average performance, as good as or better than that of half the children. (Somewhat different definitions of percentiles are given in some of the standard texts; the definition we give here is a simple one to work with and quite widely used in practice.)

To calculate the percentile rank, take the child's position* in the form and subtract it from one more than the total number in the group. In the example of the child who is 8th out of a group of 25, 8 is subtracted from $25 + 1$ ($26 - 8$), to give 18. This value is then multiplied by 100 and divided by the total number in the group, i.e. (18×100) divided by 25, giving an answer of 72. This means that the child who was 8th out of 25 is on the 72nd percentile.

The percentile rank can be obtained from the following formula:

$$\text{percentile rank} = \frac{(n + 1) - R}{n} \times 100$$

where R is position in the group counted from the top and n is the number in the group.

The percentile rank for the child who was 10th out of 27 is:

$$\frac{(27 + 1) - 10}{27} \times 100$$

$$= \frac{18}{27} \times 100 = 67 \text{ (to the nearest whole number).}$$

* With tied ranks the usual practice should be followed of referring to, say, two children sharing 4th and 5th places as equal 4th; this accords with the definition of percentiles given above. However, it is more correct to add the tied ranks and divide by the number sharing them: ($4 + 5$) divided by $2 = 4.5$; this procedure should be adopted if it is necessary to add rank orders together, or when using rank-order correlations (see Appendix C). The 'equal 4th' procedure is followed in the rest of the book.

The child who was 8th out of 25 is in fact on a higher percentile rank (72nd) than the child who was 10th out of 27 (67th).

When groups with large numbers of children are involved it is convenient to calculate only a few of the values and to interpolate the rest from a graph (see pp. 126–8).

Percentiles are useful for the purpose of comparing results in different subjects, or different aspects of the same subject. They should not, however, be added together because the tendency for marks to be distributed unevenly throughout the scale means that the difference, for example, between the 80th and 90th percentiles cannot be assumed to be the same as the difference between the 70th and 80th. For comparing results between different groups, percentiles should be used only if the groups have shared a common assessment (the same test, examination, etc., uniformly marked) or if it is certain that the groups are parallel in ability and attainment.

Scaling marks by means of a graph
Marks can easily be converted to some standard scale by using a graph. The same method can be used to convert marks from a working total of, say, 80 into a percentage (and simultaneously to convert to a standard scale, if desired) or to adjust the marks of a teacher in a department whose standards are felt to be severe or lenient.

As an illustration, let us suppose we have ten pupils' marks (out of 80) and we wish to convert the marks into percentages on a standard scale. We shall assume that the scale to be used is one with three fixed points: the top mark is to be 90 per cent, the lowest 10 per cent and the *median* score to be 50 per cent.

The median is the mark at the mid-point of the list, i.e., there is an equal number of pupils above and below it. The median is easier to find than the mean, since it involves only splitting the pupils into two groups, and, if the marks are symmetrically distributed, the mean and median should be at the same place. Usually there is not very much difference between the two.

The marks that we shall consider are:

$$68, 63, 55, 52, 48, 41, 39, 38, 34, 30$$

Since there is an even number of pupils the median comes *between* the marks of two pupils. The mark which divides the list in half is the one half-way between the fifth and sixth marks, i.e. 44·5.

On a sheet of squared paper (see Figure 10) a scale from 0–100 should be marked along the bottom and from 30–70 (the range actually used) along the left-hand side. The point (shown A) is marked, corresponding to 68 on the left-hand scale and 90 per cent on the lower one. As the median is half-way between the marks of the fifth and sixth pupils, the point B, corresponding
124

to 44·5 on the left-hand scale and 50 per cent on the lower is marked. Finally, the point C, corresponding to 30 marks and 10 per cent (the lowest score) is marked. Lines joining C to B and B to A are drawn. The values for the intermediate marks can now be read off the graph directly.

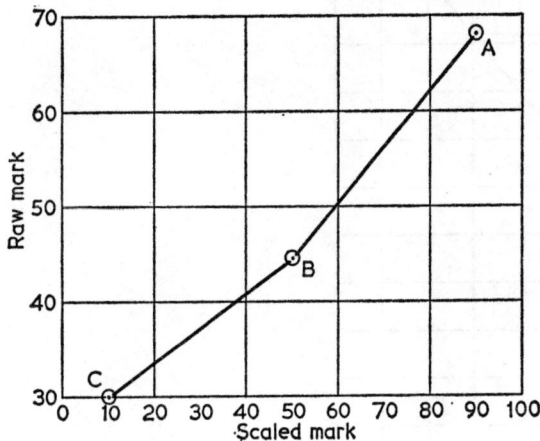

Fig. 10 Graph for the conversion of raw marks into standard scale marks

It is advisable, particularly if large numbers of marks are involved, to work down the list in order and to record each scaled mark in turn; this helps to prevent misreading of the graph.

The choice of a scale from 10–90 is, of course, quite arbitrary, though it may often be found that some subjects (e.g. mathematics) fit such a scale without adjustment.

Working with the top and bottom marks may mean that calculations can be affected by freak results. The same graphical method can be used to scale marks to equal mean and standard deviation or to the same mean and semi-intersextile range; in these cases, the fixed points on the graph are the mean and the values of the upper and lower sextiles (or one standard deviation above and below the mean). The marks being considered for this example are:

$$68, 66, 60, 58, 55, 54, 53, 51, 49, 48, 46, 44$$

The mean of these marks is 54·2 and the semi-intersextile range is 10: we shall scale the marks to a mean of 50 and a semi-intersextile range of 20. The marks are plotted as shown in Figure 11 and the scaled marks become:

$$74, 70, 60, 57, 52, 50, 48, 43, 38, 36, 30, 26$$

125

(The mean of these marks is in fact 48·7; this is quite close enough to the required value of 50, bearing in mind that it is the spread of marks which is likely to be important.) It may occasionally be found that the top or bottom mark

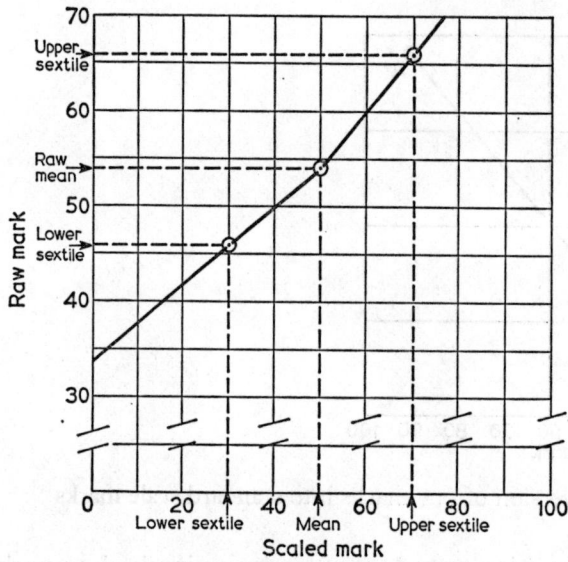

Fig. 11 Graph for the conversion of raw marks into standard scale marks, with a given mean and intersextile range

after scaling to equal mean and semi-intersextile range exceeds 100 or is less than 0; should this occur, these marks must arbitrarily be put down or up to the maximum or minimum of the scale. Because these will tend to be freak results, it is unlikely that very many marks will be involved.

Using cumulative frequencies and percentiles
To convert positions in class into percentile ranks it may be more convenient, when large numbers are involved, to use a graphical method also. Because we may get many tied ranks with larger numbers, it is easier to adopt a different method of classification and work from the *frequency* of the scores.

Suppose we have marks for a group of 30 pupils on a scale from 0–10; it is obvious that there must somewhere be numbers of children sharing the same mark and rank order. Instead of writing out the names in order, we write down

126

all the possible marks, as shown in Table 7a, and then fill in the frequency (f) with which each mark occurs. Thus we can see that no children got 10 or 0; 1 child scored 9, 2 scored 8, and so on.

Table 7a   Marks (out of 10) and the frequency (f) with which they occur in a class of 30 ($n = 30$)

Marks	Frequency of occurrence (f)		
10	0		
9	1		
8	2		
7	4		
6	5		
5	6		
4	5		
3	3		
2	3		
1	1		
0	0		

Next, starting from zero, we work out the *cumulative frequency*, i.e. the total number of children with a given score or less (see Table 7b). We see that 1 child has a score of 1 mark, 4 children (3 + 1) have 2 marks or less, 7 (3 + 3 + 1) have 3 marks or less, and so on.

Table 7b   Frequencies from Table 7a converted into cumulative frequencies and percentages

Marks	f	Cumulative f	Percentage
10	0	—	—
9	1	30	100
8	2	29	97
7	4	27	90
6	5	23	77
5	6	18	60
4	5	12	40
3	3	7	23
2	3	4	13
1	1	1	3
0	0	—	—

Lastly, the figures in the cumulative frequency column are converted into percentages (the value in the cumulative frequency column is divided by the total number of pupils and multiplied by 100). The percentages are also the percentile ranks. A score of 6 out of 10, for example, puts a child on the 77th percentile.

With a longer mark scale, it is necessary to calculate only a few of the percentages; if these are plotted on a graph, the intermediate values can be read off directly. Taking the same figures as before, the marks are entered along the bottom of the graph and the percentage cumulative frequencies (percentile ranks) along the side (see Figure 12). It can be seen, for example, that a mark of $6\frac{1}{2}$ would correspond to the 85th percentile, while a mark of $2\frac{1}{4}$ would be nearly on the 15th percentile.

The characteristic S-shaped curve, or *ogive*, will be noted; this shape is likely to be found when marks are converted into percentiles, though uneven distribution of marks (bunching at one end, for example) will cause it to be distorted.

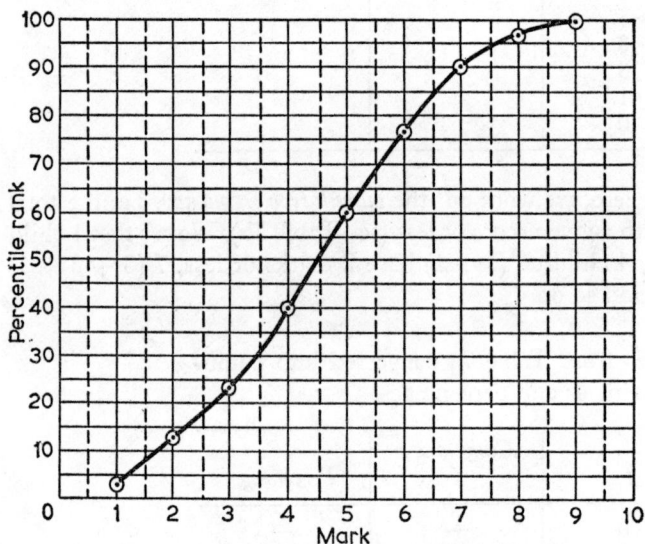

Fig. 12   Graph for the conversion of marks (out of 10) into percentile ranks

Turning marks and rank orders into grades

The precise nature of the grade scale used is of less importance than the principle that it should be applied in the same way by all teachers in a school rather than being a matter of individual whim. A short grade scale (e.g. A, B, C) is more likely to be used to the full, but, on the other hand, makes it more critical into

128

which one of the grades a child is placed. A longer scale means more borderlines although they become less important: the difference between B and C on a five-point scale is less significant than it is if there are only three grades. But some people are reluctant to use the extremes of a longer scale, as has already been mentioned in Chapter III, p. 68 and Chapter IV, p. 101.

In the interests of ensuring some sort of comparability between the grades given by different teachers, it seems essential that a uniform system is developed. One method is to award grades on the rank order within the group (either the whole year-group or within each class if they are of parallel ability) as follows:

A to the top 10 per cent of pupils
B to the next 20 per cent of pupils
C to the middle 40 per cent of pupils
D to the lower 20 per cent of pupils
E to the lowest 10 per cent of pupils

This will approximate to a 'normal distribution' (see Chapter VI, pp. 142–3), which means, roughly speaking, that one expects to get comparatively fewer extremely able or extremely weak children in a group and the majority of pupils will be clustered around the middle.

Another method is to identify the median and the upper and lower sextiles; grades can be awarded as follows:

A to pupils in the top $\frac{1}{6}$ of the group
B to pupils below A but above the median
C to pupils below the median but above D
D to pupils in the lower $\frac{1}{6}$ of the group

With an odd number of pupils, the median will have to be placed in either B or C.

It may be objected that a method which allocates an arbitrary proportion of grades as suggested above is potentially unfair since it does not allow for the possibility that a class may be better at one subject than another or that one class may in fact be of a higher standard of ability than another supposedly parallel group.

There is a certain amount of justification for such reservations and we would recommend that there is always a degree of flexibility in any scheme in order to allow for particular circumstances. However, it is easy to be misled into thinking that a group is exceptionally able simply because the children are particularly good-natured and co-operative, or because last year's group was especially bad. We would urge, therefore, that if any departure is to be made from the usual method of allocating grades, the teacher should be able to produce evidence of higher (or lower) attainment than normal to justify it.

Two methods of using a common test to identify differences between teaching groups (in the same subject) and of adjusting the standard of marks accordingly, are given in Chapter VI, pp. 134–9.

Between subjects, the situation is much more complicated; differences in attainment may be caused by the possibly inherently greater difficulty of one subject compared with another, by the particular aptitude of one class for a particular subject, by the effectiveness of different teachers or by a combination of factors such as these. The complexity of the possible interaction between these factors is so great that it is probably not sensible to try to disentangle them. The only comparatively stable factor is the group – by and large, it will be the same children who are taking the different subjects. It seems safest to assume that, unless there is strong evidence to the contrary, the attainment of the group as a whole will be roughly similar in all subjects and that grades should therefore be allocated in a similar fashion; this will be most justifiable, of course, where grades are awarded to a whole year-group rather than within each class.

Summary of Chapter V

The mark resulting from any assessment procedure is only an approximation to the true score. When adding raw marks, attention must be given to the spread of the marks as well as to the mean score. The spread is usually measured by the standard deviation of the marks; an estimate can be made by calculating the semi-intersextile range. Similarities between mark lists are measured by the correlation coefficient; unless the correlation is reasonably high, it is probably more sensible to retain separate assessments rather than trying to combine marks. Raw marks can be scaled, converted into rank orders or percentiles, or turned into lettered grades by a number of quite straightforward methods.

Questions on Chapter V

(Outline answers are given in Appendix A.)

1   Given the following set of marks (out of 120) for a class of 20:

A	75	F	82	K	51	P	87
B	96	G	80	L	115	Q	71
C	43	H	48	M	79	R	57
D	39	I	91	N	83	S	82
E	90	J	109	O	60	T	63

i   Express them as a rank order.
ii   What is the mean score? Identify the upper and lower sextiles and the median. What is the value of the semi-intersextile range?

iii Allocate grades A–D on the basis: A to the top 20 per cent of pupils, B to the next 30 per cent, C to the lower 30 per cent and D to the lowest 20 per cent.

2 The marks for the same group on another test (maximum 60 marks) are as follows:

A 43	F 51	K 25	P 47
B 56	G 22	L 48	Q 19
C 16	H 20	M 26	R 15
D 17	I 29	N 33	S 47
E 58	J 40	O 38	T 32

i   Calculate the correlation between these marks and those in question **1**.
ii Turn the second set of marks into percentages with a mean of 50 and a semi-intersextile range of 20.
iii Convert the rank order into percentile ranks.

Assignments

1 Obtain sets of *either* course-work and examination marks *or* marks from an essay test and a short-answer test in your own subject. Compare the mean and range of marks in each. Would any change in the overall order have occurred if the marks had been standardized to equal means and ranges before totalling?
2 Compare the marks given to the same class by teachers of different subjects. Calculate means and ranges as before; work out the correlation between different subjects. What conclusions can be drawn from these calculations?

Suggestions for further reading

GRIFFITHS, S. R. and DOWNES, L. W. *Educational Statistics for Beginners.* Methuen Educational, Education Paperbacks, 1969.
(A very straightforward introduction. The text is arranged in the form of a series of study units which introduce the basic language of statistics before moving on to more advanced concepts.)
HANSON, E. L. and BROWN, G. A. *Starting Statistics.* Hulton Educational, 1969.
(Attractively presented and covers a lot of ground. Intended as a school textbook.)
LEWIS, DAVID GARETH. *Statistical Methods in Education.* University of London Press, 1967.
(A more advanced reference book, but comprehensible to non-specialists.)

MCINTOSH, D. M., WALKER, D. A. and MACKAY, D. *Scaling of Teachers' Marks and Estimates*. Oliver & Boyd, 1962.
(Particularly valuable on methods for dealing with the comparatively small numbers of an average school.)

NUTTALL, D. L. and WILLMOTT, A. S. *British Examinations: Techniques of Analysis*. National Foundation for Educational Research, Slough, 1972.
(Contains much valuable information and discussion of topics such as reliability, item analysis, etc. It is very technical in parts and is not recommended for those without a sound basis in mathematics.)

Secondary School Examinations Council. *The Certificate of Secondary Education: an Introduction to Some Techniques of Examining* (Examinations Bulletin No. 3). HMSO, 1964.
(Includes sections on reliability and validity, devising an examination paper, course-work assessment, moderation methods, etc. Contains a useful statistical section dealing with mark distributions, correlation, scaling, item analysis and methods of comparing marks between teacher and moderator.)

VI. Standardizing marks – analysis of test results

This chapter is very much a continuation of Chapter V. We shall look at two methods of using a test as a moderating instrument and then at methods of analysing test results so as to find out how the test has been working.

Standardizing marks for different teaching groups

We have already referred several times to the difficulties of ensuring comparable standards of marking among several teachers in a department. If assessment is made entirely on course work, for example, is a difference in marks between one class and another attributable to a real difference in ability between the groups, or is it caused by a difference in the teachers' standards of marking?

One way of finding out if this is the case and correcting it is by arranging for the different groups to share a common test which is then used as a moderating instrument to align the teachers' assessments to similar standards. This procedure rests on the assumption that, if there are real differences between the standards of work of the different groups, these will be shown on the common element, the test that they all share. On the other hand, some children do well on tests and others do not; for this reason, we may not wish to rely entirely on the test result but to include also assessments which were made during the term.

The two methods of standardizing which are outlined below both retain the rank order of the course-work assessment while using the common tests to assimilate these assessments on to the same scale. Thus, while the marking standards have been adjusted using whole groups as a basis for comparison, within each group the individual children are unaffected, relative to one another.

The two methods are also applicable to the situation where one group takes an easy optional paper and another takes a hard one while both groups take a third common paper. The methods can also be used to standardize marks on parts of an examination which have been marked by different teachers against another part which has been objectively marked (or marked by one teacher).

Two points must be made clear: first, the common test has a lot of work to do, so great care must be taken to make sure that it is as good a test as it is possible to make; it must be both valid and reliable. Secondly, either method is justifiable only if the common test and the other assessment are, broadly speaking, measuring the same things; a correlation of around $+0.7$ would normally indicate an acceptable degree of similarity. It will be remembered that with a correlation of

+0·7, there can still be considerable disagreement about individual children – we cannot simply substitute one set of marks for another without risking unfairness to those children who have been unlucky on one occasion. And of course, even with a very high correlation, the *standard* of marking may be different, e.g. marks of 9, 8, 7, 6 and marks of 6, 5, 4, 3 would be perfectly correlated.

To illustrate the two methods, we shall use the figures given in Table 8a for two groups, X and Y, each of five pupils. Both sets have a course-work mark out

Table 8a   Course-work and test marks for groups X and Y, each with 5 pupils ($n = 5$)

Pupil	GROUP X Course work	Test	Pupil	GROUP Y Course work	Test
A	29	25	F	16	21
B	38	35	G	28	24
C	40	30	H	22	33
D	25	24	I	31	38
E	32	20	J	10	17
Mean	32·8	26·8	*Mean*	21·4	26·6

of 50 and have taken the same test (also marked out of 50). It will be seen that the average mark in group X on course work is very much higher than that in group Y but the mean test mark in X is only slightly higher. How then is it possible to compare the course work of pupil I (31) with that of pupil E (32)?

The correlation between course work and test for group X is $+0·69$ and for group Y $+0·79$; it is reasonable, therefore, to use the test marks to scale the course-work assessments.

Mapping of scores
The first step is to rule out four columns on a sheet of paper (see Table 8b). In the first column, the names of group X are written *in order on the test*. In the second, the test mark is written opposite each name. The third column is for the names of group X *in order on course work*. Finally, the marks are transferred, keeping them in the same order, from the second to the fourth column. The fourth column now represents the scaled course-work marks, and this simple procedure has ensured that the group's course marks have exactly the same distribution as the test marks; this is, in fact, a very similar result to that which would have been achieved using more sophisticated methods of scaling. The same operation is then repeated for group Y. The results of the two scaling procedures are shown in Table 8b.

134

From Table 8b it can be seen, for example, that pupil E has 20 marks on the test and 25 (scaled) for course work while pupil I has 38 on both test and course work.

Table 8b   Course-work marks scaled to the same distribution as test marks for groups X and Y

		GROUP X	
			Scaled
		Course-work	course-work
Test order	Test mark	order	mark
B	35	C	35
C	30	B	30
A	25	E	25
D	24	A	24
E	20	D	20

		GROUP Y	
			Scaled
		Course-work	course-work
Test order	Test mark	order	mark
I	38	I	38
H	33	G	33
G	24	H	24
F	21	F	21
J	17	J	17

Although similar methods are used by several examination boards to standardize internal assessments, the operation may be viewed with suspicion by those who are not familiar with it. In particular, some may find it hard to accept that B's test mark, for example, has been 'taken' from him and given to C for course work.

In fact, of course, we are using B's test mark of 35 only as a way of showing the upper limit of group X's ability, just as E's 20 forms the lower limit. It is then reasonable to fit in group X *on course-work order*, between these limits; bearing in mind that the mark is only a rough indication that the child's true score is somewhere in that region, it seems reasonable also to distribute the group's scaled course-work marks between the upper and lower limits in the same way as they were distributed on the test.

Because we have ensured exactly the same distribution of test scores and course-work assessments, the two sets of marks can now be added together as they stand, the course work can be weighted at 2:1 (3:1, etc.) against the test or, indeed, the test marks can be discarded since they have served their purpose in scaling the course marks.

Assuming that we want to give equal weight to test and course work, the combined totals for both groups are as shown in Table 8c.

Table 8c Combined test marks and scaled
course-work marks for groups X and Y

Group X		Group Y	
⌠B	65	I	76
⌡C	65	⌠G	57
A	49	⌡H	57
E	45	F	42
D	44	J	34

The composite order for the two groups would be:

1	I	76	6	A	49
2 = ⌠B		65	7	E	45
⌡C		65	8	D	44
4 = ⌠G		57	9	F	42
⌡H		57	10	J	34

Combining of rank orders
This method was devised by J. K. Backhouse* of the University of Oxford.

It differs from the mapping method in that the decision as to the relative weighting of course work and test has to be taken before the operation is started.

Using the same lists as before for groups X and Y (Table 8a), let us assume that again we want to give equal weight to both components. We must ensure that the raw scores for test and course work have roughly the same spread of marks before they can be added.†

In group X, the standard deviation of the course marks is 5·56 and for the test, 5·19; for group Y, the corresponding figures are 7·68 and 7·76. These are close enough to allow us to total the marks without first having to scale them.

The first step is to add the raw scores in the two groups to give a combined

---

* J. K. Backhouse, 'Determination of grades for two groups sharing a common paper', *Educational Research*, **XVIII** (November 1975).

† As was mentioned on p. 111, this procedure is not always enough to ensure the correct weighting; in cases such as this, with only two components intended to carry equal weight, ensuring the same spread will probably be entirely adequate.

total mark which is written out in order, as shown in Table 8d. (If the test marks are not to be counted, this step is omitted, and only the course marks in order would be written down. If the course marks were to be weighted, say, at 2:1, then they would all be doubled, after scaling, and before being added to the test scores.)

Table 8d Rank order of groups X and Y
on totals of raw scores

Group X		Group Y	
B	73	I	69
C	70	H	55
A	54	G	52
E	52	F	37
D	49	J	27

The next step is to rule two columns on a sheet of squared paper and to mark in the scale for the test marks (0–50 in our example). In the left-hand column, mark in a dot for each *test mark* scored by a pupil in group X; in the right-hand column, a dot for each *test mark* in group Y. It is convenient (though not essential) if the names of each group are written in order on total marks outside their respective columns (see Figure 13).

Working down the two central columns, it will be seen that the highest mark on the test in the two groups is 38; this is in group Y, so the first place in the combined rank order goes to the first child (on total marks) in group Y – that is to pupil I. The next highest is in group X, so second place goes to pupil B. Third highest is H in Y; fourth and fifth are both in X, and so on.

The final combined order for groups X and Y is:

$$
\begin{array}{ll}
1 & \text{I} \\
2 & \text{B} \\
3 & \text{H} \\
4 & \text{C} \\
5 & \text{A}
\end{array}
\qquad
\begin{array}{ll}
6 = \begin{cases} \text{E} \\ \text{G} \end{cases} \\
8 & \text{F} \\
9 & \text{D} \\
10 & \text{J}
\end{array}
$$

The procedure of producing a combined rank order is somewhat tedious with large numbers; if it is desired to convert ranks into grades at the end of the operation, things can be speeded up. Suppose we wanted to award grades on the basis of A to the top 30 per cent, C to the lowest 30 per cent and B to the middle band.

The overall order within each group should be prepared and the dots entered on the two central columns as before; now working down the two central

137

columns, we can say that the three highest marks on the test represent grade A (30 per cent of ten pupils). One of these is in group X (pupil B) and two in Y (pupils I and H). Similarly, the lowest three marks in the central column are 21, 20 and 17, one in group X and two in Y, so we can say that the last pupil in X

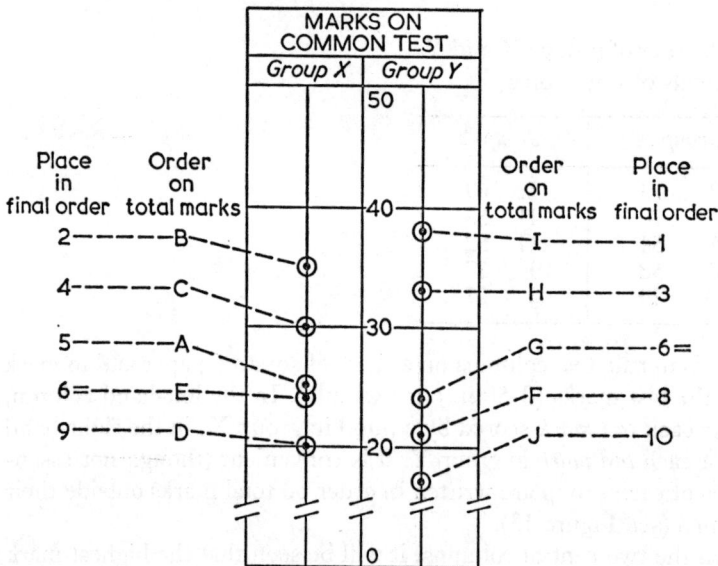

Fig. 13 Procedure for obtaining the combined rank order for groups X and Y

and the last two in Y (pupils D, F and J) will receive grade C. All that we need to know, in fact, is that a total mark of 73 in group X, or 55 and above in Y, receives grade A; 49 in X, and 37 or below in Y, receives a grade C. With larger numbers, this simplifies the operation considerably.

It will have been noticed that, although we used the same data for both methods, the final orders are not the same. This is because the mapping method preserved the differences between pupils (as shown by the intervals between the marks) and transferred them from the test to the course work. The ranking method, on the other hand, slotted one rank order into another and, as we have seen, using rank orders reduces the differences between pupils to a standard difference of one place only. With mark lists which were more closely bunched together (as when dealing with whole form groups instead of only five children) it would probably be the case that differences between the two methods would be less noticeable. Where broad grades are to be given it is also likely that minor differences in the orders will be less important. In fact, grading the final order

138

resulting from the mapping method on the same basis as we did on p. 137 (A to top 30 per cent etc.), it will be seen that the same children would receive the same grades.

The question still remains as to the advantages and disadvantages of the two methods. There is, indeed, little to choose between them; the ranking method has the advantage that the order within each group may be based on both sets of marks, thereby making use of both sources of information. On the other hand, to combine the marks may mean that they first have to be scaled. The mapping method discards the course marks and uses only the course order but automatically ensures an identical distribution of course and test marks.

The choice may be made on purely practical grounds: if one wants a total mark at the end, then the mapping method will give one; the ranking method will not. If one wants to give grades to a combined rank order, the ranking method is probably quicker, particularly if one is not counting the test marks as part of the final total.

Either method is, of course, suitable where there are more than two groups involved, provided they all share some common assessment.

Standardizing marks for groups not sharing a common paper
To standardize marks between different groups it is clear that *something* must be common. If it is not possible to arrange for a common paper, then steps must be taken to ensure that teachers' standards of marking are similar, by trial markings, discussion of criteria and sample re-marking as suggested in Chapter III, pp. 66–72. If this is done, it may be found that there is general agreement on standards and no further action is needed, though, as we warned above, it should not be assumed that agreement exists just because colleagues have participated in a trial marking – the assumption should be verified. If it is found that standards are not completely in line, it may be necessary to scale the marks of one or more teachers.

An alternative is to allocate grades in fixed proportion to each group, or to convert marks into percentile ranks, as was suggested in Chapter V. In this case, the assumption is that it is the ability of the different groups which is the same, i.e. that they are truly parallel sets. Again, the assumption should be checked; a common test can be set from time to time, classes or sets of work can be exchanged between colleagues, or standardizing meetings can be arranged to ensure common marking standards.

All in all, it is probably best not to rely wholly on any one method but to use an appropriate mixture, depending on particular circumstances. We would stress again, however, that it is not always easy for people to recognize that they are subject to the inevitable inconsistencies of human judgement; checks and balances should be built in to the system whenever possible.

Analysis of test results

We have already looked at some techniques that can help in the analysis of results: calculating the mean, finding the median, the range of the marks and the correlation coefficient. If a test is to be used as a moderating instrument, it is particularly important that results should be scrutinized closely so that we can find out how it is working, and improve it if necessary. In addition, a careful analysis can often provide the teacher with diagnostic information concerning the children's strengths and weaknesses. Some fairly straightforward methods of analysis are discussed below.

Distribution of scores

Let us take, as an example, the list of marks given in Table 9 for a class of 25 on a short-answer test of 30 questions.

Table 9 Marks (out of 30) on a short-answer test for 25 pupils ($n = 25$)

Pupil	Mark	Pupil	Mark	Pupil	Mark	Pupil	Mark	Pupil	Mark
A	17	F	25	K	15	P	14	U	18
B	26	G	17	L	14	Q	3	V	10
C	13	H	19	M	5	R	26	W	23
D	19	I	9	N	24	S	28	X	19
E	8	J	29	O	21	T	12	Y	21

Simply looking at the marks as they might be recorded in alphabetical order in the mark book does not tell us very much. Writing them in rank order makes it easier to see what has been happening:

1	J	29	13	U	18
2	S	28	$14 = \begin{cases} A \\ G \end{cases}$		17 17
$3 = \begin{cases} B \\ R \end{cases}$		26 26	16	K	15
5	F	25	$17 = \begin{cases} L \\ P \end{cases}$		14 14
6	N	24	19	C	13
7	W	23	20	T	12
$8 = \begin{cases} O \\ Y \end{cases}$		21 21	21	V	10
$10 = \begin{cases} D \\ H \\ X \end{cases}$		19 19 19	22	I	9
			23	E	8
			24	M	5
			25	Q	3

By inspection, it can be seen that the class is quite well spread out over the mark range, though there is some bunching in the middle, a situation which is fairly common. Nobody has got full marks and nobody has got zero, so the test was reasonably suitable for this group.

Interpretation can be made easier if results are expressed graphically. Bearing in mind that differences of one or two marks are probably not significant, it is handier if the scores are grouped into convenient units, i.e. in groups of three marks, 1–3, 4–6, 7–9, etc. Figure 14 shows the marks grouped in this way along

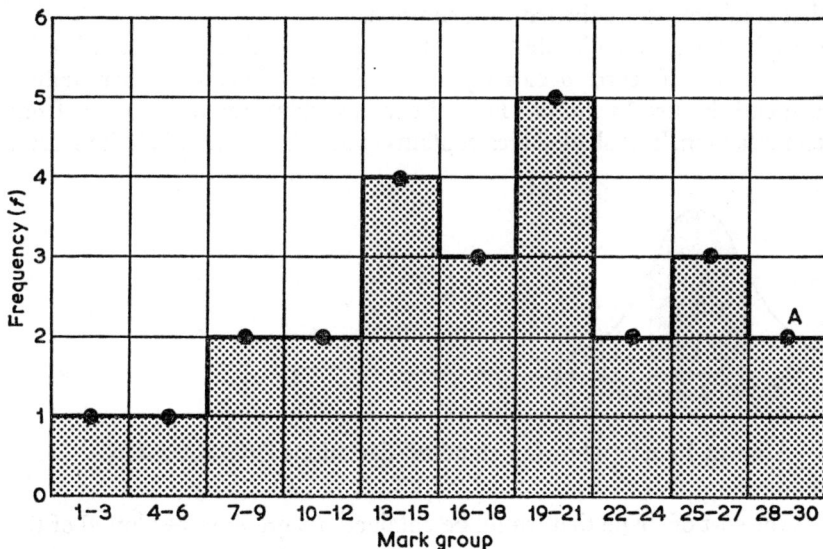

Fig. 14 Histogram showing the frequency (*f*) with which the marks in
Table 9 occur in various mark groups

the bottom of the graph; the left-hand side shows the frequency (*f*) with which scores occur in each of the mark groups. For each mark group, a dot is placed in the middle of the line which shows the number of children in that group; two children have scored between 28 and 30, so the dot marked A is inserted. The areas of the columns under the dots are shown shaded in to give a *histogram* or *block graph*. Alternatively, the dots may be connected by straight lines to make a *frequency polygon*.

We must be careful not to read too much significance into the results from one small group of children; if the test were given to a whole year-group or if results for the same test used for several successive years had been collected together, it would almost certainly be found that the irregularities in the graph would begin to smooth out. It might be found that the shape of the graph was approximating to a *normal curve*.

Normal distribution

'Normal' is used as a term of art and it does not imply that distributions of scores which differ from the normal are in any way freakish or unsatisfactory. The normal distribution is defined mathematically and is one where just over 68 per cent of the marks are within one standard deviation above and below the mean; it has been found that many attributes are distributed among the whole population in a way that conforms to mathematical definition.

On a graph, the normal distribution is shown as a bell-shaped curve, with the greatest frequency of scores occurring around the middle and numbers tailing off at each end. Figure 15 shows a normal curve, with standard deviations from the mean marked in. The shaded area contains about 68 per cent of all the scores.

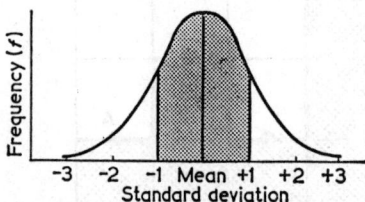

Fig. 15 A normal curve, showing standard deviations from the mean

This is the sort of shape that would be obtained if a graph were plotted of the heights of a large number of children, or of their weights, or of their speeds of running; that is to say, the graph would show most people clustered around the average, with a few people outstandingly tall or short, fat or thin, fast or slow. It is also the shape that would result if a large number of weighings of the same object was made on a crude balance.

If IQ scores or reading ages, etc. were plotted on a graph, it would be found also that something approaching a normal curve would result. *This is because the test has been designed to make it happen.* It seems a reasonable assumption that mental abilities are distributed normally, in the same way as physical attributes, but it is an assumption and there is no way of proving or disproving it. Working from this assumption, the makers of IQ tests etc. usually construct them in such a way that, if a large number of children is tested, the results will give a normal distribution.

The words 'large number' are important; within a single school, or within one class in the school, there is no guarantee that such a distribution would occur.

The normal curve gives us a basis for comparison if test scores are plotted on a graph. But we should stress again, it does not mean that scores must come out like this; the test can be made to give any distribution that is desired.

Bimodal distribution
If, for example, we had to make a pass/fail decision at around the middle of a mark range, a test which gave a normal distribution would not be very helpful because we would find, at this point, the largest number of borderline candidates. A bimodal (or double-humped) distribution would be much more effective (see Figure 16).

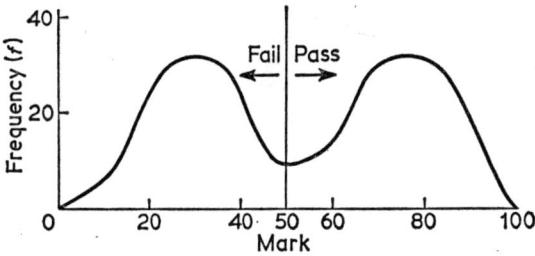

Fig. 16 A bimodal distribution

The *modal* is the most frequently occurring mark; in Figure 16 we can see that the largest numbers occur around the marks 30 and 75 and at the critical pass/ fail mark the numbers involved are much lower.

On the other hand, for the purpose of promoting or demoting children from one set to another, the normal distribution would be suitable because it spreads out the extremes of the ability range.

Skewed distribution
Marks which bunch towards one end of the scale are said to be skewed. Figure 17a is a histogram of the marks (out of 10) on a mastery test for a group of 60

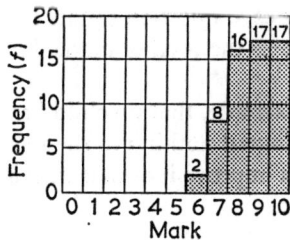

Fig. 17a Histogram showing a negatively skewed mark distribution

children. The histogram shows that, out of the group of 60, 50 have scored 8 out of 10 or better and only 10 have got less than this. The marks are said to be *negatively skewed*. The histogram in Figure 14 shows a slight negative skew indicating a test which is tending to be on the easy side.

On the other hand, if *positive skew* were obtained (see Figure 17b), it would show that the test was too hard or that the group had not covered the work properly. A positively skewed distribution might be looked for if it were necessary only to pick out a few very able children (e.g. for a scholarship) and there was no need to discriminate finely among the rest.

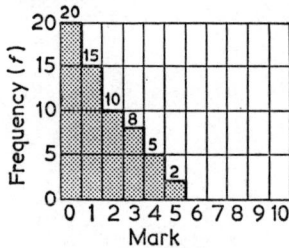

Fig. *17b* Histogram showing a positively skewed mark distribution

Question analysis

The next step in the analysis of a test to see how it has been working is to study the effectiveness of each individual question.*

Three columns should be ruled on a sheet of paper as shown in Figure 18; the first is for the number of the question, the second is for tallies showing the numbers of children answering each question correctly and the third is for the total of correct answers to each question.

When all the papers have been marked, they are gone through again (the order does not matter) and a tally is entered in the centre column for each time a given question has been answered correctly. The totals of correct answers for each question are shown under the frequency column, and if each question counts for one mark, the total for this column should be the same as the total of marks for the whole group.

By looking at the totals under f, it can be seen, for example, that no child has answered question 2 correctly; it has, therefore, contributed nothing to the test and can be discarded, unless it is felt that rewording can improve it or that with a larger number of children somebody might get it right.

---

* This sort of analysis is applicable only to short-answer, or objective-type tests, which are marked on a right/wrong basis.

Similarly, questions 10 and 11 have been answered correctly by only a few children and should also be scrutinized closely. Before deciding to delete any question, however, one must make sure that a low or zero rate of correct responses is due to a poor question and not to the group's failure to understand a point which has been covered during the term. It might be, for example, that questions 2, 10 and 11 were all on the same topic and the failure to answer indicates to the teacher that this part of the work must be gone over again.

Question	Number of correct answers	Frequency (f)
1	ⵑⵑⵑ ⵑⵑⵑ ⵑⵑⵑ ⵑⵑⵑ II	22
2		0
3	ⵑⵑⵑ ⵑⵑⵑ ⵑⵑⵑ ⵑⵑⵑ IIII	24
4	ⵑⵑⵑ ⵑⵑⵑ ⵑⵑⵑ	15
5	ⵑⵑⵑ ⵑⵑⵑ ⵑⵑⵑ ⵑⵑⵑ I	21
6	ⵑⵑⵑ III	8
7	ⵑⵑⵑ ⵑⵑⵑ III	13
8	ⵑⵑⵑ ⵑⵑⵑ ⵑⵑⵑ	15
9	ⵑⵑⵑ ⵑⵑⵑ ⵑⵑⵑ ⵑⵑⵑ IIII	24
10	ⵑⵑⵑ	5
11	III	3
12	ⵑⵑⵑ ⵑⵑⵑ III	13
13	ⵑⵑⵑ ⵑⵑⵑ ⵑⵑⵑ III	18
14	ⵑⵑⵑ ⵑⵑⵑ ⵑⵑⵑ	15
15	ⵑⵑⵑ ⵑⵑⵑ II	12

Total: 208

Fig. 18 Question analysis chart for a 15-item test with a class of 24
($n = 24$)

Questions such as numbers 3 and 9, which have been answered correctly by all the children, also contribute nothing to the discriminating power of the test, but there may be good reasons for retaining them. First, it is usually considered advisable to include some easy items, particularly early on, so that everyone can get off to a good start. This also helps to ensure that no child is likely to get the very depressing mark of 0.

Secondly, if one is going to include some questions which are intended to be answered correctly by everyone, it is sensible to set them in such a way that they form a sort of internal mastery test – in other words, to set them on some key topic in the term's work which it is expected that all the children will have

145

grasped. Failure on this internal sub-test would again provide the teacher with important diagnostic information about individual children. It is not necessary, of course, that the questions comprising the mastery sub-test are grouped together; they can be scattered randomly throughout the whole test. Questions 1, 3, 5 and 9, for example, might be a sub-test of this nature.

Much more information can be obtained if a study of the incorrect answers is made. A simple list of all the wrong answers to a question can be very illuminating and if this is done for all questions, it may be possible to see if any common pattern emerges. Similarly, listing all the wrong answers given by an individual pupil may allow the teacher to identify particular areas where that child is weakest.

This type of analysis of individual errors in a whole paper is very time-consuming and probably could not be undertaken as a matter of routine; it is, however, well worth doing occasionally because of the insights it can give into the learning process and the diagnosis of the misunderstandings of individual children.

Facility and discrimination

In order to find out in more detail how the individual parts which make up a whole test have been functioning, it is helpful to calculate two indices: those for facility and discrimination. These indices are often associated with objective tests but there is no reason why they should not also be worked out for short-answer tests (provided they are marked on a right/wrong basis); indeed, it is possible to calculate facility and discrimination values for essay-type tests as well.

The facility index (F) is defined as the percentage of pupils who answer a particular question correctly. The discrimination index (D) is a measure of the extent to which a particular question can distinguish between the most able and least able children.

Obviously the two are closely linked, but it is necessary to have both measures: questions which could only be answered by the very best children would discriminate very powerfully, but would be too hard for most of the group and possibly invalid. On the other hand, questions which everyone gets correct cannot discriminate at all.

Test constructors usually look for items with an F value of around 50 per cent (ranging perhaps from 30 per cent to 70 per cent). This does not mean, however, that all the children will get 50 marks out of 100 because, although 50 per cent will get each individual question right, it will not be the same 50 per cent each time. An F value of 50 per cent means that all the children have a fair chance of having a go at the question but that, over 30 items or so, it will be only the good ones who bring it off successfully all the time. An F value of 70 per cent

146

indicates a fairly easy question while a value of 30 indicates a hard one. It would not normally be considered advisable to include very many questions with extreme values of this sort.

The D value is usually expressed as a decimal number between -1.00 and $+1.00$. In the method of calculating it which we describe below, it is expressed, like F, as a percentage, but it can be made into a decimal simply by moving the decimal point two places to the left (e.g. D of 36·2 per cent becomes 0·36); this allows comparison with D values for published tests where D is calculated by a more complex method. Normally, D values of $+0.3$ or higher would be considered acceptable by test constructors.

It should be pointed out that F and D indices are used to construct discriminating attainment tests and the methods are not relevant where mastery testing is concerned. The purpose of including in a test only questions which have good F and D values is to refine the discriminating power of the test while keeping it at a reasonable level of difficulty. Mastery testing, on the other hand, is not concerned about discrimination between pupils, only with identifying those who have attained a certain level of competence (or better). It must also be stressed that F and D values are no more than a guide to the likelihood of a test being satisfactory; it is sometimes possible to get good values for a bad question and the teacher's professional judgement is needed to supplement the results of the analysis.

Calculating F and D values
To calculate F for a particular question, the number of children answering it correctly is divided by the total number of children taking the test, and this result multiplied by 100. The process can be expressed by the formula:

$$F = \frac{c}{n} \times 100$$

where c is the number of correct answers and n is the total number of children. Thus, question 4 in Figure 18, p. 145, has an F value of 62·5 per cent – (15/24) × 100 – while in question 6, the F value is only 33·3 per cent – (8/24) × 100.

Calculating the D value is a longer process, though F can be worked out at the same time. The marked answer sheets should be divided into three piles on the basis of total scores – a top third, the middle third and the lower third. If the number of children is not exactly divisible by three, more should go into the middle group – the top and bottom groups should be made equal in numbers even if they cannot be an exact third of the total. (There are statistical reasons for preferring to divide the papers into the top and bottom 27 per cent, and the middle 46 per cent, rather than thirds, though with small numbers this is not really worth the extra complications.)

147

A tally chart should be prepared, showing the number of the question, columns for High, Middle and Low groups, a column for totals and a column for D. Under the row for each question, a space should be left for the percentage values (see Figure 19). Working through the High group of scripts, a tally is placed in

	High	Middle	Low	Total (F)	D
Question a	⳾⳾⳾ ⏐⏐⏐ ⑧	⳾⳾⳾ ⑤	⏐⏐⏐ ③	16	
Percentage	80	50	30	53	50
Question b	⳾⳾⳾ ⏐ ⑥	⳾⳾⳾ ⑤	⏐⏐⏐⏐ ④	15	
Percentage	60	50	40	50	20
Question c	⳾⳾⳾ ⏐ ⑥	⏐⏐ ②	⏐ ①	9	
Percentage	60	20	10	30	50
Question d	⳾⳾⳾ ⏐ ⑥	⳾⳾⳾ ⏐⏐⏐ ⑧	⏐⏐ ②	16	
Percentage	60	80	20	53	40

Fig. 19 Part of a tally chart for calculating F and D values

the appropriate box for each correct answer; the process is repeated for the Middle group and for the Low group. Totals are entered inside each box and also an overall total of correct answers in the fifth column. These totals are then expressed as percentages (divide by total number in each group and multiply by 100) which can be entered in the line under each question.

The percentage value in the fifth column is, of course, the value of F. To arrive at D, the percentage in the Low column is subtracted from that in the High. For example, the value of D for question **a** is: (percentage in High column) — (percentage in Low column), i.e. $80 - 30$, giving a D value of 50 per cent or 0·50, as it is usually expressed. It can be seen that question **b** has a D value of 20 per cent. It therefore discriminates too little and would be rejected from the test; question **c** has good discrimination ($D = 50$ per cent) but might be rejected as being too hard ($F = 30$ per cent).

This method of calculating D is an approximate one; in particular, it omits to take any account of the Middle group. The percentage of correct replies in the Middle group should be somewhere between those in the top and bottom

148

groups – roughly half-way would be ideal. If the percentage in the Middle group is *above* that in the High group, or *below* that in the Low group, the item should be rejected, even though the D value as calculated is satisfactory. Question **d** would be rejected for this reason. A question with a negative value for D would also be rejected.

The method (like the more sophisticated methods which can be used) depends on the assumption that performance on the whole test (which determines the High, Middle and Low groups) is a better measure of ability than performance on any one question can be. Essentially, it estimates the extent to which each question does the same sort of job as the whole test – the correlation of each question with the whole. It is because D is a correlation that it is usually written as a decimal number with a positive or negative sign, rather than as a percentage.

Good D and F values for each question should mean that the test as a whole is of a reasonable level of difficulty and is internally consistent (i.e. all the questions measure more or less the same sort of ability) which in turn means it should be fairly reliable.

It may be found, in fact, that sufficient information about the F and D values can be obtained if the performance of each question is plotted as a histogram* (see Figure 20). A descending 'staircase' with roughly equal steps is satisfactory

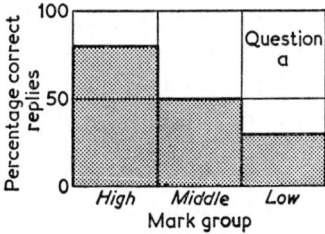

Fig. 20 Histogram showing the percentage of correct replies to question **a** in Figure 19, for High, Middle and Low groups ($n = 30$)

in terms of discrimination and if even the lowest step is of reasonable size, then it is a fair indication that the question is not too hard for the group.

Estimating F and D from a histogram or working out their values as described can help us to decide which questions should be omitted or included if we want

---

* If total numbers in the High, Middle and Low groups are exactly the same, it is not necessary to convert the numbers into percentages. Similarly, with equal numbers, D can be calculated by subtracting the number in the Low group from the number in the High group and turning this result only into a percentage. This short cut is possible only where there are equal numbers in all groups; since we have to be able to compare the Middle group's results also, where numbers are not divisible by three, we must work in percentages.

to improve a test. The two indices are most useful if the questions can be pre-tested (that is, tried out first on a sample of children of similar ability to those who will take the final version) so that amendments can be made if necessary. However, even if pre-testing is not done, analysis of the test can enable it to be improved for use next year. It must be remembered, though, that the values of F and D depend on the particular group of children who take the test and if they are especially good (or bad), the values of the indices will not be typical. Interpretation of the indices must therefore be made with such factors in mind.

F and D values for essay-type questions
The analysis given above is suitable for short-answer tests which are marked on a right/wrong basis. For questions which must be marked more subjectively, a different method must be employed.

The value of F can be calculated* by dividing the total marks given for any question by the maximum marks possible; if the answer is multiplied by 100, it will give a percentage value in the same way as we calculated F above. The formula is:

$$F = \frac{T}{M} \times 100$$

where T is the total marks obtained by all pupils on a given question and M is the total maximum marks obtainable by all pupils on that question. Thus, if a group of 5 pupils had marks (out of 10) of 10, 8, 6, 4, 2, the value of T would be $(10 + 8 + 6 + 4 + 2) = 30$; M would be $(5 \times 10) = 50$ and $F = (30/50) \times 100 = 60$ per cent.

Because we are concerned with subjective marking, a low F value may be due *either* to a hard question *or* to severe marking (or to a combination of both). Careful scrutiny is essential to decide which of these factors is the cause of the low value, and, if necessary, the severe marking should be adjusted.

The value of D can be calculated by working out the correlation between the marks on an individual question and the total marks on the whole paper (see Chapter V, pp. 112–21). It should be observed, however, that D values for an essay-type question will always tend to be higher than those for a short-answer test. This is because the essay question is usually one of a comparatively few questions on the whole paper and therefore the mark for any one question also plays a significant part in the total mark; with a short-answer question, on the other hand, each question counts for only one mark out of perhaps 30 or 40.

In conclusion, it must be pointed out that, where a choice of questions is allowed, F and D values, calculated according to the methods outlined above,

* See D. L. Nuttall and A. S. Willmott, *British Examinations: Techniques of Analysis* (National Foundation for Educational Research, Slough, 1972), pp. 22–4.

may be misleading. It is necessary to consider whether one question was chosen by a particularly able group of pupils or a group below average ability; the value F must be interpreted with this in mind and D must be calculated as the correlation between marks on a particular question and the total marks *of the group choosing that question*. As we have already said, a choice of questions complicates everything and should be avoided, if at all possible.

A cautionary note

In any statistical operation, it has been found by bitter experience that the most common sources of error are in the mechanical processes of counting up numbers, entering figures in a table, and adding and subtracting. All calculations should be checked and rechecked, in as many different ways as possible. We have indicated in the text ways in which certain checks can be made – these steps should never be omitted.

Summary of Chapter VI

A common test can be used as a moderating instrument to standardize assessments between different groups. A reasonable correlation between the common test and the other assessment is necessary for this to be justifiable and special care must be taken to make the common test a good one. Analysis of test or examination results can give an insight into the efficiency of the test and can also provide the teacher with valuable diagnostic information. Calculation of the indices of facility and discrimination will enable unsatisfactory questions to be detected and the test to be improved.

Questions on Chapter VI

(Outline answers are given in Appendix A.)

1 Two groups, X and Y, take the same paper (Z). Group X also takes a hard paper (H) and Y takes an easy paper (E). Their marks (out of 30 on all three papers) are:

	GROUP X			GROUP Y	
Pupil	*Paper H*	*Paper Z*	*Pupil*	*Paper E*	*Paper Z*
K	22	27	P	25	19
L	12	20	Q	21	11
M	25	25	R	22	15
N	18	17	S	28	21
O	9	10	T	26	17

i   Use the mapping method to arrive at a combined total mark for both groups, giving equal weight to both components. Place both groups in a single rank order. Allocate grades on the basis: A to the top 20 per cent, C to the bottom 20 per cent, B to the middle band.

ii Work out a combined rank order using the method on pp. 136–9, again with equal weightings for H, Z and E. Is this order the same as that in **i**?

2   Given the following set of marks (out of 60):

A 44	F 36	K 39	P 48
B 30	G 27	L 25	Q 42
C 41	H 58	M 50	R 21
D 56	I 32	N 33	S 34
E 50	J 44	O 40	T 45

group the scores in fives, starting at 21–25, 26–30, etc., and draw a histogram showing the distribution of scores.

3   For the first five questions of a test given to a class of 28 pupils, the following figures are obtained:

Question	High (9 pupils)	Middle (10 pupils)	Low (9 pupils)	Total (F)	D
1	7	5	3	15	
2	9	7	4	20	
3	8	3	5	16	
4	4	3	1	8	
5	5	6	2	13	

i   Calculate F and D values for each question.

ii Which questions would you reject and why?

iii Draw a histogram for each question, showing the percentage of correct answers in each group.

4 On one question of an essay paper (5 questions, each out of 20 marks) taken by 20 pupils, the marks were as follows (total marks for each pupil are in brackets):

A	19	(90)	F	14	(66)	K	9	(45)	P	6	(52)
B	18	(94)	G	13	(58)	L	9	(55)	Q	5	(27)
C	17	(86)	H	13	(40)	M	8	(62)	R	4	(25)
D	17	(71)	I	12	(67)	N	7	(70)	S	4	(38)
E	16	(82)	J	11	(49)	O	7	(46)	T	2	(33)

i Calculate F and D values for this question.
ii Comment on the values obtained.

Assignments

1 Using results from one of your school tests or examinations, draw graphs showing the distributions of marks.
2 Analyse a short-answer test in your own subject to show **a** the numbers of correct responses to each question and **b** F and D values for each question.

Suggestions for further reading

The references at the end of Chapter V cover statistical methods; the following books deal with the applications of these methods, for example to the evaluation of the curriculum or organization of the school, or to some other piece of research.

EVANS, K. M. *Planning Small-scale Research*. National Foundation for Educational Research, Slough, 1968.
NISBET, J. D. and ENTWISTLE, N. J. *Educational Research Methods*. University of London Press, 1970.

On the evaluation of the curriculum (see also Chapter VII)
Schools Council. *Evaluation in Curriculum Development: Twelve Case Studies* (Schools Council Research Studies). Macmillan Education, 1973.
Schools Council. *Curriculum Evaluation Today: Trends and Implications* (Schools Council Research Studies). Macmillan Education, 1976.
WISEMAN, STEPHEN and PIDGEON, D. A. *Curriculum Evaluation*. National Foundation for Educational Research, Slough, 1970.

VII. Assessment in the secondary school

In this chapter an attempt will be made to pull together various threads and to consider the application to the school situation of the assessment techniques which have been discussed. We shall look first at problems arising from changes in the curriculum and consider also evaluation in the context of the whole school. We shall discuss the planning of a school assessment programme, look briefly at the related subjects of school records and reports and, finally, consider the role of public examinations.

Curricular changes and problems of assessment and evaluation

Suggestions for changes in the curriculum seem to be appearing at a dizzy pace: glossy new textbooks come out almost daily, pundits fill the pages of the educational press with learned treatises on new teaching methods, innumerable conferences are held to spread the gospel according to the disciples of the latest educational messiah. Many people, despairing of being able to keep track of developments, come to regard any innovation with a jaundiced eye, and perhaps the greatest problem in curriculum development is not in designing the new course, but in ensuring that schools become aware of it and can consider its adoption.

This is not to imply that curriculum development is a waste of time, nor that it is not, in many cases, long overdue, though the length of time that a traditional syllabus or method has been in existence is not, of itself, sufficient ground for assuming inadequacy.

It is necessary to have something more than hunches to base one's decisions on; curriculum development teams will make a careful survey of the field before commencing their work and will usually include an evaluator in the team, though it should be pointed out that the evaluator's main task is likely to be one of formative evaluation (that is, leading to improvements in materials and methodology) rather than a summative, or terminal, evaluation. In addition, where the curriculum is intended for the upper secondary school, very often special syllabuses are prepared for public examinations so that pupils can obtain certificates in the normal way.

However, it must be made clear that the type of evaluation that a project team will be concerned with is (and must be) quite different from the evaluation that an individual teacher will need to carry out. At this level, evaluation

154

is an essentially personal affair: will the course suit my style as a teacher, my pupils, my school? In addition to the assessment which may be made for a public examination under the auspices of an examining board, the teacher will need to devise his own scheme of assessment for the new course in order to provide himself and others with information on his pupils' progress and attainment at various stages; he must also be able to interpret the results of these assessments, and to supplement them with information from other sources and with his own professional opinion where necessary, in order to make an evaluation of the success of the new method in the context of his own particular situation.

In Chapter I, the relationship between assessment and evaluation was defined: while assessment, in our terms, implies a measurement of children's educational attainment, evaluation is much broader and is concerned not only with attainment in a subject but also with many less definable but equally important factors such as children's attitudes towards learning, the impact of the new course on resources, and so on. Broadly speaking, it could be said that assessment is concerned with how well the child has done, but evaluation with whether it was worth doing in the first place.

Problems of assessment

The curriculum comes first, and a new course means that methods of assessment must be reconsidered in the light of possibly different aims and content. The example in Chapter IV, Table 4, of the assessment of group discussion is an illustration of the way in which a new assessment procedure has been worked out for a type of course which is in many respects radically different from the traditional concept of a school subject; the idea of an equally traditional examination (essays, written papers, etc.) for such a course would be manifestly absurd.

Fitness-for-purpose is the first consideration – why is the assessment needed? It has been shown that different methods of assessment will be chosen to provide the teacher with immediate feedback, for departmental records, for the school report. Having established the purpose of the assessment, then the more detailed considerations of fitness for this purpose must be faced: validity, in terms of aims and objectives and in terms of content, the reliability of the methods chosen, and the implications in terms of the time and resources required to carry out the programme.

We would suggest that there are five key questions which should be answered in connection with any proposed assessment:

1   Will making this assessment benefit the education of the children, directly or indirectly?
2   Is it a valid test of what they have been learning?
3   Can it be marked fairly and uniformly?

4 Will it provide, when needed, all or part of the appropriate information about the children's attainments?

5 Are there any important aspects of the course which are not covered by this assessment?

The answers to the first four questions must be 'Yes', if the assessment is to be worth carrying out. The answer to the fifth question will almost always be 'Yes', but it is an important one all the same. The tendency is to concentrate on those aspects which are assessable and the danger is that more indefinable aims or long-term goals may be overlooked in the day-to-day concern with what may, indeed, be less important, immediate objectives.

The rider to this question is: 'And what is going to be done about it?' It may be sufficient just to remind oneself of the long-term aims of one's teaching, or one may need to supplement the assessment with some additional measure, but it is important not to concentrate solely on the easily assessable.

Integrated courses
Particular problems may arise where a school has integrated some of the traditionally separate subjects into a broad humanities course or a general science course, etc.

In some cases the course might more aptly be termed co-ordinated rather than integrated in so far as subject teachers continue to teach their own specialism but the courses are focused on a common theme. The assessment procedures then require little more than a similar sort of co-ordination, for example, by consultation on form and style of examination questions, together with standardization of the marks to some common scale.

In other instances, however, there may be a greater fusion of subjects and the problems of assessment are intensified. It also becomes more important that an accurate assessment is made, since, inevitably, some aspects of such courses must be dealt with by teachers who are not specialists in one or other of the disciplines involved.

Attempting to break up a genuinely integrated course for the purpose of making a separate assessment of each component would be contrary to the principles which have been advocated throughout this book. The assessment must match the teaching and an integrated course should have an integrated assessment. The corollary is that tests and examinations for such courses must be prepared in consultation with representatives of all the disciplines involved, if an unconscious bias in favour of one's own specialism is not to creep in.

Since, by definition, a fully integrated course of this kind will be significantly different from the separate subjects it replaces, it becomes all the more important that assessable objectives are specified; this specification, too, should be prepared in consultation with members of the team.

156

Detailed mark schemes should similarly be jointly drawn up and discussions held among the team of teachers about the criteria for assessment.

It must also be borne in mind that if a teacher is unsure of himself in dealing with one particular aspect of an integrated course, he may well be equally uncertain when it comes to assessing it. Course-work assessments would seem particularly liable to suffer from this effect and the head of department should take special steps to ensure that children in the different groups are assessed on a similar basis.

Assessment in mixed-ability groups
Where a school is organized in parallel, unstreamed teaching groups, each containing virtually the whole range of ability found in secondary schools, the need for accurate assessment becomes specially important.

In a banded or streamed school, the teacher's expectation of the standard of work that he should get from any pupil will be in part conditioned by the stream or band that the pupil is in. Leaving aside the important question of how the children were divided into streams or bands in the first place, once they have been identified as able or less able, A stream or D, the individual teacher will tend to adjust the level of his work accordingly. With the mixed-ability group, however, the prime responsibility for identifying children's abilities, and for providing them with the appropriate level of work, remains with the class teacher.

The problems of any school assessment – the subjective nature of much of the assessment, the difficulty of ensuring comparable standards of judgement, the time required to carry it out and the record-keeping associated with it – are all accentuated in the mixed-ability situation.

Individual programmes of work may make it almost impossible to ensure syllabus coverage in a test where no two children have completed the same amount of the syllabus; reading and writing problems for some pupils may invalidate conventional (written) testing methods and some people feel that the philosophy of mixed-ability teaching precludes any form of competitive testing, i.e. any test which produces a rank order.

It must be observed that there can be a competitive element in any form of assessment; if the children are given any sort of mark or grade, whether it is in the form of a rank order, a percentile rank, a lettered grade, for attainment, in relation to the child's own best work or whatever, as long as there is an implication that A is better than B, then one child will be able to say he has 'beaten' another. This is probably inevitable; many children seem to have a strong competitive urge but one which can, with care, be channelled to lead to good motivation and higher attainment. It must not be overdone and too much competition would not be considered desirable in most schools; nevertheless, there are practical advantages for the teacher in rank ordering and, of course, it is not necessary that results should be given to the children in this form. When considering alternatives, halo effect should be remembered; an attempt to make a subjective assessment of a child's term's work may well be influenced by personal relationships, by unduly weighting the most recent piece of work, etc. In addition, an individual's concept of standards is likely to vary and it is hard to be sure that work of similar standard is always given the same grade.

By contrast, a child's position in the group represents a comparatively stable measure. Where the group have all shared the same learning experiences and the same assessments, the gain (or loss) of a number of places in the order may well be a better indication of a child's progress than an impression grade at the end of term.

However, this should not be taken to mean that rank ordering is the only way in which assessments can be carried out. If the children are working to individual programmes based on a work-card or work-unit system, then the course can be arranged so that it is, in a sense, self-assessing. If the course consists of a number of units, in an ascending sequence of difficulty (plus a number of revision or remedial units), then both progress and attainment can be measured by the number of units completed in a given time. 'Completed', of course, implies 'completed satisfactorily' and some courses build in a test unit to be done after completion of work on one topic to check that the material has been done properly. There is a risk with this sort of self-paced scheme that the most able children may race ahead and lose contact with the rest; many teachers would consider it advisable to pull the group together to a common starting-point from time to time and to arrange the work-units so that the abler children can work at each topic in some depth before moving on, while the slower children concentrate more on understanding the basic core material.

The type of test which would be included in this sort of scheme would be a mastery test, i.e. it would be expected that most children who had worked hard at the preceding material would score high marks. Even if a course is not arranged in work-units, a similar sort of test programme can be devised. This is normally referred to as *criterion-referenced testing*,* that is to say, each test is designed to measure attainment of a specified level of ability (the criterion) and together, the tests form a sort of staircase up which the children move one step at a time as and when they are ready; the system of standards in music examinations is a well-known example of criterion-referenced testing.

To devise a scheme of criterion-referenced tests in school requires very careful planning and could only be done where the syllabus also had been planned in such detail that what the children were expected to be able to do at each stage could be clearly specified. It may not be possible to do this at all in some sub-

* By contrast, the constructor of a discriminating test, aiming for items which will be answered correctly by about 50 per cent of the pupils, is making a *norm-referenced* test.

jects but, where it is appropriate, such a scheme (like the work-unit scheme) has obvious attractions, not least of which is that the tests are taken when the child or group is ready for them and the disruption and stress of the end-of-term examination can be avoided. In other cases, it may be possible to arrange a system of overlapping tests or examinations, as suggested in Chapter VI, pp. 133–9, using the common element to equate standards between the children who have taken the harder paper and those who are doing less advanced work, though it should be said that this, too, is not an easy task.

If no tests or examinations are to be set, then assessment must be based wholly on course work and steps must be taken to ensure that comparable judgements are made by teachers of different groups. It must be remembered that it will probably be necessary for many of the children, at some stage, to enter for a public examination and that examination technique takes a certain amount of acquiring; it will probably be thought advisable to give the children the opportunity of practising working under examination conditions if they are likely to have to take a conventional examination at a later stage.

In the above discussion, it has been tacitly assumed that the assessment will be of written work. Educational testing in this country has relied almost totally on written methods though on the continent there is much greater reliance on oral examining at all levels. In the mixed-ability group, it may well be found that deficiencies in skills of literacy will invalidate the normal test methods for some children. This is paralleled in the streamed school where it is usual to find that the lowest or remedial stream does not take part in the same examinations as the rest of the year-group. Oral examining is an obvious answer, provided that problems of time and standardization can be overcome. If it is too difficult to examine a whole group orally, and if some children are withdrawn for remedial teaching, it may be possible to conduct oral tests with this sub-group only until such time as their skills of reading and writing have improved sufficiently to allow them to rejoin the main body.

Aural testing is another possibility; even if a normal test paper is read out by the teacher, it may help the weaker children, though it may be found that the quicker pupils have finished the test before the teacher is more than half-way through the reading. If listening booths are available, pre-recorded tapes of the text could be prepared for the use of some children.

It must be admitted, however, that none of these solutions is entirely satisfactory and, in certain cases, it may have to be accepted that some children will be outside the scope of the test. It is regrettable that our measuring instruments are not yet adequate for the task that they are asked to perform, and it is to be hoped that no school would place such a premium on academic attainment that these children would not feel that there are other aspects of their school life where they can make some worth-while achievements.

Evaluation within the school

Evaluation of whether or not a school is successful in attaining its educational objectives is a matter of crucial importance to all concerned: staff, parents, and, not least, pupils. Many rather vague claims are made, for example, that vertical division into houses prevents children from feeling a loss of identity in a large school, that integrated courses foster an idea of the unity of knowledge, and so on; only rarely, however, is any attempt made to find out whether the claims are justified.

It is true that there are severe problems associated with this type of evaluation and that techniques for carrying it out are as yet hardly developed. Nevertheless, it is necessary to make a start somewhere and, even if a first attempt is unsuccessful, those involved are likely to learn much about themselves and their school in the process.

In many respects, there is a parallel with the problems of assessment; before an evaluation can be carried out, it is necessary to make explicit just what the school is trying to achieve. As with teaching aims and objectives, it is necessary to specify the school's goals with a degree of precision which will make evaluation possible. A generalized statement such as 'allowing every child to develop to his full potential' is undoubtedly praiseworthy but so imprecise as to be of little use: it is like a declaration that one is 'against sin' – few will dissent from it, until one begins to define exactly what constitutes sin in one's own morality. It is essential, at this stage, that all a school's goals are stated, even though some of them may be long-term aims, or those for which, at present, we have no valid measure available. Most schools, for example, would consider the attainment of good academic standards to be an important goal; it is certain, however, that few schools would make it the most important, or only, aim for all children. The explicit statement of what the school feels to be its educational objectives is some sort of safeguard against undue emphasis being placed on only one aspect of the total experience provided.

It will certainly be found that some of these objectives fall into the area of, using the term broadly, academic attainment – attainment of basic skills of literacy, oracy, numeracy and graphicacy, achievement of satisfactory examination grades for those pupils needing this type of qualification, the provision of sufficient courses with sufficient flexibility to suit the aptitudes and interests of individual children. Others will be in the area of social development – co-operation in group activities, awareness of the responsibility of the individual to the community, attitudes towards social problems, etc. Others will be in the aesthetic field – sensitivity and artistic appreciation, the development of purposeful and satisfying leisure activities, and so forth.

For some of these objectives, measures exist: examination results, standardized tests of literacy and numeracy. For others, evidence can be obtained: an inquiry

160

into pupils' leisure pursuits, the degree of voluntary participation in community activities, for example. And for some, no evidence may be obtainable, or, at best, we may have to rely on an intuitive judgement. A long-term goal, such as 'helping children to take their place as adults in society' is not susceptible to evaluation within the school – indeed it is doubtful whether it could be rigorously evaluated at all. But it is possible to define certain characteristics which it is hoped will lead to a well-adjusted adult life and which can be observed in pupils; this will go some little way towards a solution. Some evidence, too, on children's attitudes can be collected by using one or other of the tests or attitude scales which are available for this purpose (see references at the end of Chapter I), though some are of rather dubious validity and reliability. Questionnaires or interviews may also be used to collect information from teachers or pupils and can be valuable if the topic is one where only a subjective impression is possible. We should warn readers, however, that the preparation of a questionnaire or the conduct of an interview is far from straightforward and surprising results can be obtained by the inexperienced.

Probably the most objective attempt at evaluation within the school is the third volume (1972) of the series of reports on comprehensive schools from the National Foundation for Educational Research in England and Wales: *A Critical Appraisal of Comprehensive Education* (by J. M. Ross, W. J. Bunton, P. Evison and T. S. Robertson). In this study, investigators attempted to establish how far certain schools were successful in achieving the declared aims of comprehensive education. The authors freely admit that, in several aspects of the study, they were unable to reach any definite conclusions because of the kinds of problems which have been outlined above; nevertheless, readers who are interested in evaluation are strongly recommended to read the report because of the valuable insights it gives into the difficulties and the way in which a team of skilled researchers attempted to overcome them.

Evaluation of the subject curriculum
Evaluation of the curriculum within a department will probably be much more closely connected with the assessment of attainment in the subject, rather than is the case in the sort of evaluation that we have been discussing above.

There will, of course, be a need for evaluating pupils' attitudes towards the subject and their interest and enthusiasm for it; an attitude scale may be used, or pupils may be asked to list subjects in order of preference, or in what they consider to be order of importance, etc. This may lead to invidious comparisons between departments, however, and, although such a survey can be illuminating, it would be tactically unwise to conduct it at more than fairly infrequent intervals. Nor should too much credence be attached to the results; children's attitudes towards a subject, and perhaps their perceptions of its importance, can often be affected by the personality of one particular teacher or by current fashions in teenage culture. It may also be the case that an appreciation of the value of certain studies comes only after some years of application to mastering the fundamentals. One can hardly enjoy the game of tennis until one is moderately sure of being able to return the ball over the net and into court; similarly, children's judgements at an early stage may not be valid simply because they have not enough experience on which to base them.

Although including consideration of the less precise (though undeniably important) non-cognitive aspects, curriculum evaluation will probably be largely founded upon the programme of assessment within the department. Indeed, as shown in Chapter I, Figure 2, the teaching aims and objectives, which shape both the content of the course and the scheme of assessment, will also help to provide the criteria for evaluation. These components should be considered as a whole, not in isolation, just as the evaluation of an individual subject should be considered in the context of the whole school; however, there will be particular requirements at the evaluation stage which will make it necessary to supplement or at any rate to reinterpret the results of the normal assessment programme.

Assessment, in our definition, is mainly concerned with the progress of individual children; although there is inevitably an overlap between the two, evaluation is more concerned with the performance of a whole group.

In evaluating the course, therefore, more useful information will be obtained from looking at the performance of whole groups, at mean scores or at the percentage of children reaching a specified level of competence, for example, rather than at the variations in the attainment of one child from term to term.

It will almost certainly be necessary to obtain additional evidence on particular aspects. The use actually made of a new piece of equipment might need to be known, for example, as well as teachers' opinions on its usefulness. Similarly, the number of times children visit the school or public libraries might have a bearing on the evaluation of a course intended to develop the pupils' ability to carry out investigational work on their own.

It all depends on what the department feels it is trying to teach and a clear specification will go a long way towards clarifying problems of evaluation. We have mentioned this topic only briefly but have suggested some starting-points for those interested; readers who wish to pursue the matter further are referred to the works listed at the end of Chapter VI.

Planning a school assessment programme

The programme of assessment within the school must be designed to produce, as economically as possible in terms of staff time and resources, accurate information about the children, when it is needed, and in a form suitable for whoever needs it. Let us consider these points in a little more detail.

i *Information to be obtained as economically as possible in terms of staff time and resources*
Some of the procedures we have suggested in preceding chapters are time-consuming and some require more expenditure on materials than a test scribbled on a blackboard and answered on a scrap of rough paper. Many teachers seem to mark anything that comes into their hands by a sort of reflex action and this too takes time, though often it is not time spent to the best advantage. We would suggest that improving the accuracy of our assessment procedures should mean that we can assess less often and place greater reliance on the results; it is disheartening, to say the least, to add together a mass of term marks only to find that the end-product bears little relationship to what the teacher feels to be the children's true abilities. It is more a question of cost-effectiveness than net cost and if the assessment is necessary, then it should be done well.

But balance is essential; it is of little use devising such a sophisticated scheme that no one has time to do anything else but operate it.

ii *Information about the children to be accurate*
The reliability and validity of the test method used are of prime importance, to which must be added another factor which has already been mentioned: comparability between grades given by different teachers and in different subjects. As far as possible, the assessment procedure must ensure that a child of given ability would receive the same mark or grade, no matter when or by whom he is assessed.

iii *Information to be obtained when it is needed*
The assessment programme must be geared to the frequency of school reports or parents' meetings, to the timing of internal decisions on streaming, banding or setting and on entry to public examinations, etc.

iv *Information to be in a form suitable for whoever needs it*
The information kept in a teacher's own mark book may well be in a different form from that which will be given to the parents; information to assist in curriculum evaluation, as has been suggested above, may be of a different kind again; the house-tutor may need a different sort of information from that required by the head of department.

Consideration must also be given to the use that may be made of standardized tests, whether of IQ, reading ability, numerical ability, or standardized attainment tests in a subject, if available (see pp. 15–19). Some people have advocated

163

plotting attainment grades in relation to IQ scores or some other indicator of academic ability, so that it can be seen whether a child is over- or under-achieving in relation to his potential. This is dangerous ground and opinions differ strongly; others would argue that making use of test scores in this way leads to lowered expectations for the children who do not do well on the test, and thus to diminished attainment, making the test a self-fulfilling prophecy. Much doubt has been cast on the validity and, indeed, the usefulness in schools, of IQ tests* and, in view of the complexity of the debate on this topic, it seems wiser to suggest that scores from such tests should be regarded as offering no more than supplementary information to that obtained by other means.

Another debatable point is the assessment of attitudes (interest, enthusiasm, effort) and personality. Some would argue that effort, interest, etc., if well directed, must lead to higher attainment and that it is neither necessary nor desirable to assess them separately; others would want to see some recognition for the child who has worked hard, though perhaps reaching only a very modest standard.

Each school will decide which of these arguments carries greater force; we would urge, however, that if an assessment is to be made of any aspects of a child's education, it should be based, at least in part, on observable manifestations of the child's behaviour. Effort, in a global sense, is not observable and an attempt to assess it is liable to interference from the old enemy, halo effect. Thus, it would be necessary first to specify how interest or effort might be displayed in each subject and then to observe how far each child displayed it. One might well have to supplement such evidence by an overall impression (because of the difficulty of making a complete specification) but it seems likely that an assessment based on some evidence, even though incomplete, will be sounder than one based on little more than personal feelings.

It is important to remember that children's attitudes can change very rapidly, much more so than their attainment, and that in attempting to assess something which is unstable, we may be attempting the impossible. Children may give misleading answers, either in an attempt to please the teacher, or to give an answer which is acceptable to their contemporaries, or they may genuinely believe that they have certain attitudes to a problem which to them exists solely in abstract terms, only to find that they feel quite differently when faced with the reality of the situation.

In particular, children may be guarded in their replies if an attempt is made to probe deeply into certain sensitive areas of the personality.

There may, indeed, be real dangers in such an attempt and it has been shown that the results of such an investigation, even when conducted by trained psy-

* For example, see D. A. Pidgeon, 'The interpretation of test scores', *Educational Research*, **IV** (November 1961), 33–43.

chologists, are often inconclusive and may be misleading.* We would recommend, therefore, that the teacher should confine himself largely to aspects of the personality which have a direct bearing on educational achievement: interest, enthusiasm, etc., such as may properly be the subject of comment in the end-of-term report, and leave the more profound investigations to those trained to carry them out.

Some teachers may wish to introduce into the programme an element of self-assessment by the pupils. One important aim of the school must be, indeed, to develop the child's awareness of his own strengths and weaknesses and to encourage self-assessment (and self-evaluation) in this sense. Some work done at the Bosworth College† shows that encouraging pupils to write a report on themselves to the teacher can provide valuable feedback. It is clear, however, that this procedure is unlikely to assist in the assessment of attainment, in the strict sense (though it may help in evaluation) since pupils cannot, by definition, be in possession of sufficient knowledge and experience to make an objective appraisal of their standard of work.

Though intended to supplement, rather than replace, examination results, school assessments and reports, etc., the Swindon Record of Personal Achievement‡ is worth mentioning at this stage. Over a period of two years the pupil compiles a folder containing records of any achievements he considers to be worth including, which may be sporting activities, social service, his attendance record, out-of-school activities such as Scouts or Guides, part-time employment, school visits, or, indeed, examination results. All that is necessary is that each record is countersigned by an adult who knows the facts to be true. In this way, the pupil compiles a very personal record of what he has done and one which can tell a prospective employer, for example, a lot about him.

Coming back, however, to the topic of assessment, whatever aspects it is decided to include in an assessment programme, it should be planned in conjunction with the system of record-keeping in the school.

School records and reports

Just as with assessments, it is important to strike the right balance in a school's system of records. It is possible to devise an extremely comprehensive and sophisticated record system, but if the staff cannot find the time to keep it up to date, it will be of little value. Nor is there much point in keeping detailed records of

* For example, see Philip E. Vernon, *Personality Assessment: a Critical Survey* (Methuen, Social Science Paperbacks, 1969).

† D. Marcus, *Reports and Reporting* (Bosworth College, Desford, Leics., 1973).

‡ Information about the Swindon Record of Personal Achievement can be obtained from The Organizer, Curriculum Study and Development Centre, Sanford Street, Swindon.

dubious assessments – the records can be no better than the information they contain.

There will be problems if it is attempted to make the school's central records too comprehensive: information will become lost in a mass of material. Equally, problems will arise if the records are inadequate to provide the right sort of information when needed.

A possible solution to the dilemma is to attempt a degree of decentralization in school records, with records at several levels, so that information in increasing detail can be obtained should the occasion arise. This is the sort of organization that is adopted in some large schools, with a greater devolution of responsibility for record-keeping to heads of divisions, heads of houses, year-tutors, etc., while the central record remains as a summary. Much of the information which is recorded is obtained by the class teacher from his normal assessments of homework and classwork, examination results, etc. It seems logical, therefore, to start at the beginning with the teacher's mark book.

Mark books

One of the odder aberrations of our educational system is the view that a mark book is the personal and private property of the individual teacher, which he organizes entirely as he sees fit and which he takes away with him when he leaves the school. Particularly with the increased rate of turnover of staff it seems ludicrous that potentially important information about the children should be lost in this way.

There is a simple answer to the objection that nobody else but the teacher responsible can know how to interpret the marks in the book: the mark book should be arranged so that the information is immediately comprehensible to any other teacher in the department. This implies that departments should organize the keeping of mark books in such a way that a standard layout is observed. Obviously, the particular procedure adopted will depend on the subject concerned and the demands of the school for information for central records, reports, etc.; nevertheless, a few basic principles can be suggested as a starting-point.

i   *Marks from different types of assessment should be kept separate.*
That is to say, there should be separate sections for marks for homework, classwork, tests and examinations. This will make it easier to see, for example, that homework is being done regularly or if there is a discrepancy between the standard of homework and classwork for any one pupil; also, if any set of marks has to be scaled, it is easier if they can be dealt with en bloc.

ii *Marks for different types of work should be kept separate.*
If a department regards one aspect of the subject as being distinct from another then it is sensible to keep the marks distinct also. Thus, the modern language department might wish to keep separate marks for oral work, free composition, translation, etc.

iii *The work which has been marked should be clearly identified.*
The date of marking and the nature of the work done should always be shown in the mark book. Where tests are involved, particularly if they are shared by a whole year-group, or if they are part of a scheme of criterion-referenced testing, it will be helpful if the tests are given a code letter or number for easy reference.

iv *The criteria for assessment should be clearly understood.*
In particular, it should be made clear whether the assessment is for attainment or for effort. If it is thought desirable to include a grade for effort, interest, etc., it should be in a separate section from attainment marks; ways should be worked out in which the amount of effort shown by the children can be observed, and space allowed for recording this assessment. Additional space should be left, as required, for the conversion of total marks into grades or for scaled marks, for the prediction of public examination grades, and the actual results, for the form order, if any, for records of books studied by pupils or project work under-taken, and so on. It would also be advisable to allow space for a comment oppo-site each child's name relating to any relevant circumstances, such as prolonged illness, a bereavement, behavioural difficulties, etc., which may have affected performance at any time. It is also useful if a record is kept of the comments written on the child's report which can aid later interpretation of marks or grades.

It would, of course, be possible to transfer such information to special cards and to file them away at the end of each term, thus allowing the teacher's mark book to remain sacrosanct. However, this would involve the tedious chore of copying records from one source to another, with the inevitable possibility of errors and omissions. It seems more sensible to regard the teacher's mark book as the first school record and, perhaps by using a loose-leaf system, to file the relevant pages at the appropriate time. This suggested procedure would involve some changes from what seems to be the normal practice of keeping personal mark books. It implies that the mark book should be part of the whole school system of records, that it should be arranged in such a way that it contains the information that the department and the school may require and that it is avail-able to professional colleagues who may need to consult it.

Departmental records
Depending on the organization of any particular school, it might be that the department acts as the repository for first records, in the sense outlined above.

167

In addition, however, the department will probably be concerned with curriculum evaluation in the broadest sense, including both evaluation of the appropriateness of the course and of the effectiveness of the teaching of different groups. Provision should therefore be made for additional records showing results of questionnaires, mean test scores, examination grades, etc. (see pp. 161–2) as well as for records of individual children's attainments.

Departmental records will, of course, also need to include stocklists of equipment, stationery, etc., but these are outside the scope of this book.

Pastoral records

Pastoral records are also outside the scope of this book and all we would wish to say on this topic is that in a number of schools there appears to be a serious dichotomy between academic and pastoral records. A positive effort should be made to ensure the exchange of information between the two 'sides', which are not really sides at all, since the school as a whole will be concerned with the development of the child as a whole, and not with separate and distinct aspects of his education; in particular, all information must be available to the class tutor who forms a vital link in the communication chain.

Central records

For administrative convenience and efficiency, we have urged that the school's central record should be a summary of what is detailed in other records. Thus, a department may wish to retain a profile assessment, with separate grades in different aspects of the subject, while the central record contains a single overall grade. In this way, a query from, say, a parent concerned about a child's progress or a prospective employer who wants details of attainment can be answered at any level of generality as appropriate to the inquiry.

Depending on the use of such tests in the school, central records might also contain details of scores on standardized tests; information from the primary school, on family background, medical history, and so on, may also be included. It is important that all members of staff should be aware of what information is contained in the records and have access to it when necessary.

School reports

School reports come in for regular and often justified criticism. Too often they convey little real information to parents and, on occasions, what information there is can be positively misleading.

It is undoubtedly important to supplement reports by interviews with parents but this is not, in our view, an excuse for an inadequate report in the first place. The interview should be a discussion, based on the information in the report, not a lesson in how to interpret cryptic (and sometimes illegible) comments or meaningless grades. If marks or grades are to be given on the report at all, then parents should be in no doubt as to how to understand them; it should be made quite clear whether they are for effort or for attainment, and what the criteria are by which they are awarded. Further, it should be made clear that grades are, or are not, comparable between different subjects, that a grade A in English means the same sort of ability in that subject as does an A in mathematics. If this cannot be done, then it should be explained that Mr So-and-so's B is really just as good as Miss Such-and-such's A. This may be embarrassing, but it is, after all, only an accurate reflection of the situation which probably exists if no attempt is made at standardizing marks.

The frequency of reporting is a matter for careful consideration, bearing in mind the severe strain imposed on staff and balancing this against the right of parents to be informed about their children's progress.

It is suggested that it is probably most satisfactory if a fairly flexible system is devised, with a full report perhaps once a year, supplemented by short reports at more frequent intervals, and with the timing of full reports being staggered for different year-groups. In any case, it would probably be desirable to make sure that parents can request a special report at any time if a child's progress is causing concern. It may also be found advantageous to vary the frequency and the nature of reports between upper and lower school; in particular, parents may need fuller information as the time approaches to consider subject options and entries for public examinations.

It seems unfortunate, however, that parents are rarely consulted on school reports, since they are the main consumers, and it would be useful if more was known about what the parents wanted and what sort of interpretation they place on the information they receive at present.

Public examinations

Public examinations have been with us for a long time and, although, at the time of writing, there is much talk of changes to the system, it seems likely that they will be with us, in one form or another, for some time to come.

Examinations come in for a lot of criticism from people who ascribe to them all the ills of education; perhaps it is sometimes overlooked that they can exercise a useful regulating function for the schools in curbing some of the wilder extravagances of educational experimenters, and that they provide a means by which most children can obtain accreditation of their attainments regardless of where they are or what school they attend. Nevertheless, public examinations need watching. Experience in the past has shown only too clearly how the examination syllabus can become the teaching syllabus and what a sterile and restrictive effect this can sometimes have on the schools.

Examining boards nowadays are very conscious of their responsibilities in this respect and control of the syllabus is in the hands of serving teachers so that the examination tends to reflect generally accepted practice rather than to dictate what must be taught. Nevertheless, and in spite of the efforts of the members of the boards' subject advisory panels, there is an in-built tendency in most examinations towards maintaining the status quo. This, we believe, is caused by the absence of a specification of the examination of the sort we outlined in Chapter III. Although there are exceptions, it is still more often than not the rule that the examination is specified in terms of the syllabus content, the method of examining and past papers. Of these, past papers are by far the most important factor.

Since there is too often little more guidance for the teacher than a list of topics, and a note of the duration of the examination, he has virtually no choice other than to study past papers to get an idea of the sorts of things the examiners are likely to ask. This, in turn, acts as a powerful constraint against the examiners to try anything different, and to overcome the resulting tendency towards ossification needs a conscious and continuing effort.

The move towards stating aims and objectives in examination syllabuses is a welcome one, though at present it may be suspected that in some cases such statements have merely been tacked on to an existing content-based syllabus which has remained virtually unaffected by the worthy sentiments expressed at the beginning. In the model which we have been advocating, the aims and objectives shape the syllabus content and thence the scheme of assessment. The content is therefore purely functional, the servant of the aims and objectives, while the scheme of assessment measures the attainment of the objectives, again using the syllabus content only as a means to an end.

We would see, too, the move towards direct testing of skills and ideas, rather than just factual knowledge, as one which is compatible with our model and one which is likely to lessen the tendency of examinations to become stultified. The use of primary source material in history examinations to test historical skills of interpretation and comprehension, rather than merely the recall of lists of dates and Acts of Parliament, is one example, as is the introduction of problem-solving tests of practical skills in the sciences. The fact that the trusted techniques of question-spotting and rote-learning can no longer be relied upon in such examinations is, in our opinion, a positive advantage educationally, and a direct consequence of the clear specification of teaching aims.

Another factor which has encouraged the development of examinations in recent years is the opportunity for schools to devise Mode III examinations; that is to say, examinations set and marked by the school but moderated by an examining board, which, when satisfied that standards are comparable with those of its own (Mode I) examinations, will issue the normal certificate to the pupils.

The facility for choosing a Mode III examination has undoubtedly helped schools which wish to experiment with a new slant on an accepted subject or to introduce a new subject into the curriculum.

There has been a steady growth in the number of Mode III examinations and it would be fair to say that this has brought a number of problems both to the boards and to the schools.*

The boards have the responsibility of ensuring that Mode III is not a soft option and that demands are made on candidates similar to those that are made in Mode I. Techniques of moderation are still in a comparatively early stage of development and there are many difficulties yet to be overcome. It seems, however, that there is a general acceptance that the Mode III school-based examination is a necessary and desirable option, and that growth is likely to continue.

For the teacher, preparation of a Mode III scheme involves a considerable amount of work, both in the initial submission of the scheme for consideration by the board and in setting and marking the papers, and/or carrying out other assessment procedures.

Different examining boards have different procedures and it will usually be found that a small handbook giving guidance to teachers preparing Mode III schemes is available. This should be studied carefully; not only must regulations about the dates of submissions, numbers of copies of syllabuses, etc. be carefully observed, but it will also be found that much useful information on examining techniques and methods of moderation is included. It will also be helpful to establish personal contact as soon as possible with the member of the board's staff or the moderator responsible for dealing with the subject so that difficulties on either side can be ironed out.

It seems strange that the other mode of examining is not made more use of: Mode II examinations are set by the board on the school's syllabus, thus allowing the school to devise its own course but relieving the teacher of the problems associated with setting the paper. Obviously, a Mode II would be impracticable in a scheme based largely or entirely on intermittent assessment during the course, but where there is a terminal examination it would seem that Mode II can offer some real advantages to the teacher.

It may seem, in view of what we said in earlier chapters about the test fitting the teaching, that *only* a Mode II or Mode III examination could be acceptable in our terms. However, the distinction between the board's examination and the school's is no longer as clear-cut as it used to be. In many Mode I examinations, there is a substantial proportion of internal assessment; the 'pure' Mode I – a wholly external examination – is tending to become something of a mixture, with

* For further discussion of this topic see Schools Council Examinations Bulletin 31, *Continuous Assessment in the CSE: Opinion and Practice* by Roland Hoste and Barbara Bloomfield (Evans/Methuen Educational, 1975).

elements of Mode III creeping in. In any case, we qualified our earlier dictum by saying that a test might be chosen to suit the teaching rather than having to be devised to do so. Just as the teacher may find that a standardized test may meet his requirements, so he may find that an external examination syllabus is sufficiently close to what he considers should be taught to be acceptable. And since, as we have said, the board's subject panel will have devised it with this in mind, it is not surprising that this should be so.

Conclusion

Since Chapter VII has been very much a summary of what was in the rest of the book, there is no summary of this chapter. We have attempted to suggest various lines of follow-up to the many aspects of the subject where there is more to be said or where the present state of the art is still undeveloped, and it is hoped that readers will be encouraged to investigate further. If there is a single moral to be drawn from this book, it probably is 'Take nothing for granted'. It applies, of course, to what is contained in this book; we do not claim to have found any final answers but we would hope that we have provided a starting-point from which people can begin to work out their own solutions.

Suggestions for further reading

On the philosophy of examinations

Secondary School Examinations Council. *The Certificate of Secondary Education: Some Suggestions for Teachers and Examiners* (Examinations Bulletin No. 1). HMSO, 1963.
(Contains important sections on this topic.)

WISEMAN, STEPHEN (ed.) *Examinations and English Education.* Manchester University Press, 1961.
(The fundamental work on the philosophy of examinations and their relationship to the curriculum.)

On evaluation in the secondary school

ROSS, J. M., BUNTON, W. J., EVISON, P., and ROBERTSON, T. S. *A Critical Appraisal of Comprehensive Education.* National Foundation for Educational Research, Slough, 1972.

On the historical background to public examinations

BRUCE, GEORGE. *Secondary School Examinations: Facts and Commentary.* Pergamon Press, 1969.

(Contains a review of developments in examinations and some interesting suggestions for the future.)

MONTGOMERY, R. J. *Examinations: an Account of Their Evolution as Administrative Devices in England.* Longmans Green, 1965.

(Contains a very comprehensive survey of the development of public examinations from about the middle of the last century to the present time.)

Appendices

Appendix A   Outline answers to questions

Answers to questions on Chapter I

1 The first step would be to study the syllabus for the external examinations; if a sizeable mark allocation was given for field work then there would be little cause for concern. If this was not the case, the teacher would have to show that field work was important as a way of learning, i.e. that understanding of geographical concepts was improved by practical experience in the field and that these concepts were tested in the external papers. This might be done by small-scale pilot studies, e.g. by comparing the ability to read maps with a class which has done practical work relating a map to the actual location and one which has only had classroom experience. After the teaching programme had been in operation for a few years, there would also be the opportunity of studying the actual examination results, but before introducing his new programme on a large scale, the teacher should certainly try to find out, by some small experiments, what its effects are likely to be.

Alternatively, he might be able to show that geography teaching confined to the classroom was not meeting an important educational aim, such as developing an awareness of the environment. Not all teaching aims are examinable and some things are worth doing even if they do not bring a pay-off in terms of certificates.

2 The written papers can test theoretical knowledge. Before accepting the assessment one would have to know the teaching aims: if theoretical knowledge was the only (or the most important) aim, written papers might be acceptable. If, however, the teacher's main aim was to help the children acquire practical skills, then written papers might give quite misleading results; in this case, the teacher would do better to carry out a continuous assessment of practical work during the term.

3 **a** Probably not, at any rate not without some addition. There is no mention of the candidates' ability to recall facts which would almost certainly be a factor in the essay paper and the objective test, though, of course, not relevant to project work.

b No. Section **iii** says the project must be in a readable form. The tape-recordings would have to be transcribed, on a literal interpretation of the rubric;

it is possible, however, that by readable the history panel meant comprehensible and that, without wanting specifically to exclude tape-recordings, it simply had not occurred to them that they might be used. The wording of this sort of statement must be very carefully considered.

The question is also an example of an unfair technique in that it seems to focus on the subject of the project (Education before 1914) and the method of investigation (interviews with old people), both of which are acceptable in terms of the panel's statement; in fact, of course, the question is aimed at the word readable and the use of tape-recordings. (Trick questions are dealt with further in Chapter II.)

Answers to questions on Chapter II

1 The distribution of the marks is bunched badly towards the lower end of the scale: 14 children have scored 5 out of 20 or less. It would be a reasonable conclusion that the test is too hard for this class. Further, if any children are to change streams following this assessment, the test would be quite inadequate for this purpose, particularly at the bottom end. Discrimination between the last three children and the four next lowest is a matter of a single question right or wrong. To conclude that this represents any real difference in their ability would be unjustifiable. The severe bunching means that the test is unfit for the purpose of helping to decide promotions and demotions. Ideally, a test for this purpose would bunch the middle band together but spread out the extremes, top and bottom.

2 The validity of a half-hour test of a year's work must be suspect; it is unlikely that syllabus content could be sampled adequately and half an hour will not permit assessment of those skills (essay writing etc.) which require time to test. In addition, the time interval between examinations is so long that feedback on children's progress will be very infrequent. The implication is that the individual teacher should carry out an assessment of course work throughout the year in order to supplement the information he will obtain from the test. (Course-work assessment is mentioned in Chapter IV and a method of combining test scores with those from course work in Chapter VI.)

3 Regular tests of this nature have more of a teaching function than anything else. They are a form of mastery test and, if successful, they should show a lot of high scores. If the end-of-term examination is also a mastery test, then totalling the weekly scores should give a similar result. However, if the end-of-term examination is intended to discriminate, then the mastery tests will not achieve this purpose.

4 Coverage of the factual content of the lessons could be quite good with this test and reliability also should be reasonably high. However, it would not be easy to test in this way understanding of the interaction of the many factors involved and it would be necessary to supplement the short-answer test by some other method (such as essay writing, discussion, etc.) in order to make a fuller assessment of the extent to which the teacher's objectives had been achieved.

Answers to questions on Chapter III

1 Aim **i** is all-embracing and not specific enough to help in specifying the examination except in so far as it indicates that opportunity should be given for children to demonstrate the scientific way of thinking, e.g. by forming hypotheses, collecting evidence, evaluating it, etc. Aim **ii** is not really relevant to examination matters, though obviously important to the teacher. Aims **iii** and **iv** imply a large amount of practical work (see Chapter IV) together with written work involving the recording and interpretation of results. Interpretation could also be tested partly in a written paper, where the children are given the data and asked for an interpretation.

2 This question can be answered by virtually any native speaker of English, even if he is unfamiliar with Lewis Carroll's work. The reason why it *can* be answered (even though the meaning of the words is unknown) is that a native speaker can identify the 'verbs' (gyre and gimble) from their position in the sentence and the syntactic clue 'did' before them. The question, therefore, is testing recognition of the sentence structure of English and the syntactic markers of the English verb. This is confirmed in the answer where gyre and gimble have the verbal suffix 'ing' attached. It is then a purely grammatical question, with no intrusion of semantics. Why one might want a purely grammatical question, without any meaning, is, of course, quite another matter.

3 The procedure depends crucially on members of the department giving the same grade to work of similar standard; the most critical points will be the A/B boundary and the D/E boundary. In fact, if B, C and D are going to be grouped together, there is little point in giving three grades within this group. The head of department should try to standardize marking at the A/B and D/E levels, with discussions of sample scripts and trial markings, if possible. He should also review borderline pupils himself, taking into account other evidence (course work etc.) in doubtful cases. He would also review periodically the composition of the sets after the examination in order to make transfers between sets where appropriate.

Answers to questions on Chapter IV

1 Because this is a crash course, the pupils will be progressing from zero knowledge to (it is hoped) a reasonable standard in a comparatively short time.

177

Assessments in the early stages will therefore tend to bear little relationship to the attainment of the pupils at the end of the two years. It would be wise to make no assessments of oral ability (or at any rate, none that will count towards the final grade) during the earlier part of the course. Those assessments that are made later should also be more heavily weighted than the earlier ones in order to take account of the pupils' progress.

2 The procedure is most probably invalid; most teachers of home economics would want to cover more than simply cookery, and even within cookery many would consider choice and selection of ingredients to be important. Moreover, concentrating on a single test of this nature can have unfortunate (and possibly unfair) results; if a child encounters some disaster in the cooking, the whole meal may be spoiled and there is no chance to redeem oneself on another occasion. The equal weighting given to the preparation sheet and the final meal is suggestive more of suiting the examiner's convenience than validity in assessment; a meticulously written preparation sheet but a badly cooked meal will not satisfy many appetites!

3 The vital consideration in assessing a group project is whether individual pupils' contributions can be separately assessed. If not, a weak member of the group may be carried by the rest. Where production of a play is concerned, very careful consideration is needed as to the relationship between attainment in the subject and ability in stage management, histrionic talent, etc. It could easily happen that the assessment is inadvertently made on quite different grounds from that for pupils doing more conventional projects.

4 If the parents have no more information than is given here, the results cannot be interpreted at all. Even if it is known, for example, that the child is in the middle band of a streamed comprehensive school, they are not much more meaningful. The grade B for science may mean that the term's work was much better than the examination work or that the examination was severely marked or that the teacher wanted to encourage a child who was not doing very well. The English teacher may give nothing higher than B; the mathematics teacher may allocate grades precisely according to the numerical total of term marks. If the child is in different sets for each subject and marks and grades are given in relation to each set (so that a B in the bottom set for geography represents a lower standard than a C in the top history set) the situation is even more chaotic.

It is obvious that the parents must be able to supplement this sort of report by personal interviews with the staff concerned. However, this is not, in our opinion, a reason for some schools to continue to issue inadequate and often misleading information to parents and pupils.

Answers to questions on Chapter V

1 i The rank order is:

1	L	115		11	M	79
2	J	109		12	A	75
3	B	96		13	Q	71
4	I	91		14	T	63
5	E	90		15	O	60
6	P	87		16	R	57
7	N	83		17	K	51
$8 = \begin{cases} F \\ S \end{cases}$		$\begin{matrix} 82 \\ 82 \end{matrix}$		18	H	48
				19	C	43
10	G	80		20	D	39

ii Mean = 75·05; upper sextile = 94·33; lower sextile = 49; median = 79·5; semi-intersextile range = 22·67. (The standard deviation of these marks is 20·44.)

iii L, J, B, I get grade A; E, P, N, F, S, G get B; M, A, Q, T, O, R get C; K, H, C, D get D.

2 i By the HILO method, the correlation is $+0·71$.

ii Rounded off to the nearest whole number, the scaled marks are:

E	80	A	61	M	40	C	28
B	77	J	57	K	39	R	26
F	71	O	55	G	35		
L	67	N	48	H	33		
$\begin{cases} P \\ S \end{cases}$	$\begin{matrix} 66 \\ 66 \end{matrix}$	T	47	Q	31		
		I	44	D	29		

The standard deviation of these marks is 16·9. (The graph for the conversion is given in Figure A.1, p. 180.)

iii The percentile ranks are (using the formula on p. 123):

E	100	A	70	M	40	C	10
B	95	J	65	K	35	R	5
F	90	O	60	G	30		
L	85	N	55	H	25		
$\begin{cases} P \\ S \end{cases}$	$\begin{matrix} 80 \\ 80 \end{matrix}$	T	50	Q	20		
		I	45	D	15		

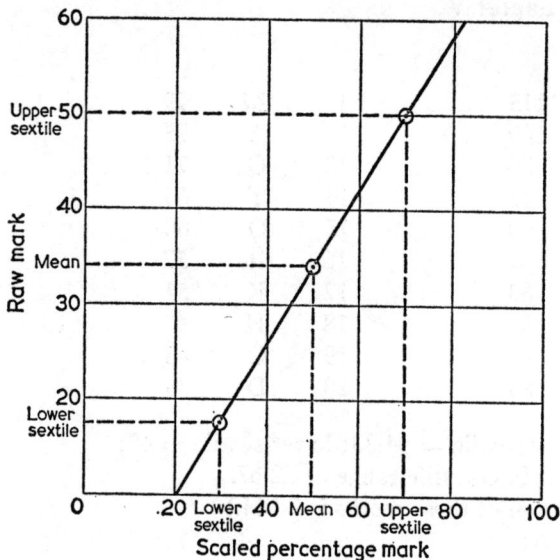

Fig. A.1 Graph for the conversion of raw marks into scaled percentages (answer to question **2ii** of Chapter V)

Answers to questions on Chapter VI

1 i The combined rank order and total marks are:

$$1 = \begin{cases} K & 52 \\ M & 52 \end{cases} \qquad 6 = \begin{cases} T & 36 \\ P & 36 \end{cases}$$

$$3 \quad S \quad 42 \qquad\qquad 8 \quad R \quad 30$$

$$4 = \begin{cases} L & 37 \\ N & 37 \end{cases} \qquad\qquad \begin{array}{ccc} 9 & Q & 22 \\ 10 & O & 20 \end{array}$$

K and M receive grade A;
S, L, N, T, P, R receive grade B;
Q and O receive grade C.

ii The rank order is (working on raw totals, without scaling):

$$\begin{array}{ll} 1 & M \\ 2 & K \\ 3 & S \\ 4 & N \\ 5 & P \end{array} \qquad\qquad 6 = \begin{cases} T \\ L \end{cases}$$

$$\begin{array}{ll} 8 & R \\ 9 & Q \\ 10 & O \end{array}$$

180

It is not the same as in **i** though grading on a similar basis would give the same result.

2 The histogram is shown in Figure A.2.

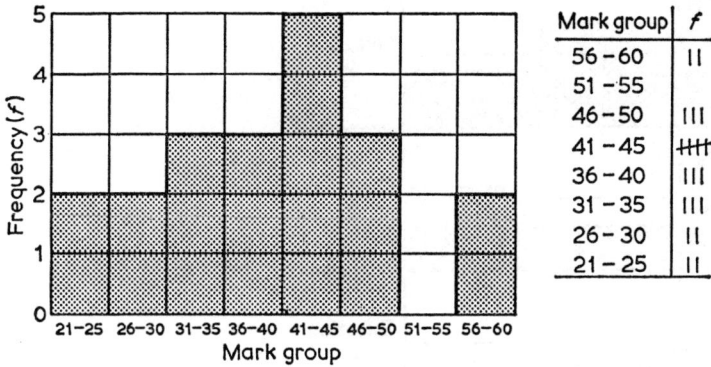

Mark group	f
56–60	II
51–55	
46–50	III
41–45	⊦⊦⊦
36–40	III
31–35	III
26–30	II
21–25	II

Fig. A.2 Histogram showing the frequency of occurrence of marks in various mark groups (answer to question **2** of Chapter VI)

3 i The values (to the nearest whole number) are:

Question	High	Middle	Low	F	D
1	78	50	33	54	44
2	100	70	44	71	56
3	89	30	56	57	33
4	44	30	11	29	33
5	56	60	22	46	33

ii Question 3 would be rejected, because of the higher value in the Low column than in the Middle.
Question 4 is doubtful because of the low F value.
Question 5 would be rejected because the Middle value is higher than that in the High column.

iii The histograms are shown in Figure A.3, p. 182.

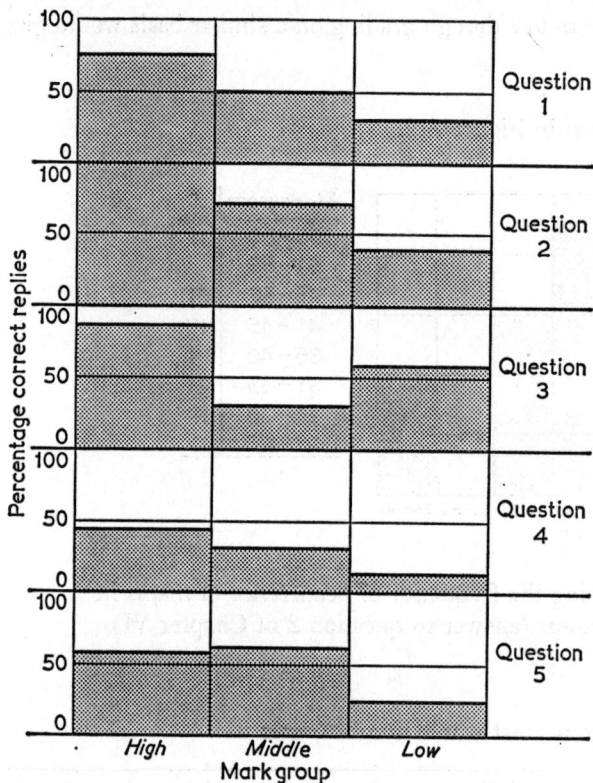

Fig. A.3 Histograms showing the percentage of correct replies in High, Middle and Low groups to 5 questions (answer to question **3iii** of Chapter VI)

4 i The total mark on this question is 211; the maximum possible is $20 \times 20 = 400$.

$$F = \frac{211}{400} \times 100 = 52{\cdot}75$$

By the HILO method, $r_p = 0{\cdot}71 = D$. (Note: on the marks for the question, there is a gap at the mid-point at 10 marks; the arrows are placed on either side of the gap, at 9/10 marks and 10/11.)

ii These values indicate a fairly satisfactory question.

Appendix B Criteria for tests of discrimination, conformity and standards

The values for the three tests given on page 7 of Schools Council Examinations Bulletin No. 5 are for a CSE scale of 5 grades plus an ungraded category (6 grades in all).

To convert to another grade scale:

1   the test for discrimination remains the same;
2   the value (12) for the test of conformity must be converted by multiplying it by the number of new grades and dividing by 6; e.g. for 5 grades, the value becomes $(12 \times 5)/6 = 10$;
3   the value (10) for the test of standards must also be multiplied by the number of new grades and divided by 6; e.g. $(10 \times 5)/6 = 8.3$.

If raw marks in percentages are used, it is recommended that they are converted into broad grades (perhaps 10 in all) before applying the three tests.

Appendix C   Correlation formulae

Spearman's rank-order coefficient (ρ)
This is calculated using a fairly straightforward formula:

$$\rho = 1 - \frac{6 \times \Sigma d^2}{n(n-1)(n+1)}$$

where Σd^2 is the sum of the squares of the differences between the two rank orders and n is the number in the group. Tied ranks should be given the average place (two tying for 3rd and 4th places $= 3 \cdot 5$) with this method.

Pearson's product – moment correlation (r)
The basic formula is:

$$r = \frac{\Sigma x_1 x_2}{n(\sigma_1 \sigma_2)}$$

where σ_1 and σ_2 are the standard deviations of the two sets of marks, $\Sigma x_1 x_2$ is the sum of the products of the two sets of marks, *expressed as deviations from the two means*, and n is the number in the group.

Modifications to this formula are needed for grouped marks, etc. Readers are referred to the works listed at the end of Chapter V.

The HILO method – a note by G. F. Peaker
The justification of the HILO procedure is that in a very large normal bivariate population we have the relation $r = \cos(1-p)$, where r is the correlation co-efficient and p the proportion of the population that lies in the positive quadrants of the defining axes through the centroid. This is the relation tabulated and graphed in Figure 6, p. 119. In samples drawn from the population the relation holds approximately, the approximation being close for large samples but increasingly rough as the sample size diminishes, and also as the parent population departs from normality. In the kind of application illustrated in the text, experience shows that the odds are about two to one that the discrepancy will not exceed $0 \cdot 06$.

General bibliography

This list includes all books and articles referred to in the text as well as other relevant publications.

BACKHOUSE, J. K. 'Determination of grades for two groups sharing a common paper', *Educational Research*, **XVIII**, November 1975.

BLOOM, B. S. (ed.) *Taxonomy of Educational Objectives: the Classification of Educational Goals*, Handbook I: Cognitive Domain. Longmans Green, 1956.

BRUCE, GEORGE. *Secondary School Examinations: Facts and Commentary*. Pergamon Press, 1969.

BURNISTON, CHRISTABEL. *Creative Oral Assessment*. Pergamon Press, 1968.

BUTCHER, H. J. *Human Intelligence: Its Nature and Assessment*. Methuen, University Paperbacks, 1970.

DAVIES, ALAN (ed.) *Language Testing Symposium: a Psycholinguistic Approach* (Language and Language Learning Series). Oxford University Press, 1968.

DYSON, A. P. *Oral Examining in French*. Modern Language Association, 1972.

EBEL, ROBERT L. *Essentials of Educational Measurement*. Prentice-Hall, 1972.

EGGLESTON, J. F. *A Critical Review of Assessment Procedures in Secondary School Science*. Leicester University Press, 1965.

EGGLESTON, J. F. and KERR, J. F. *Studies in Assessment*. English Universities Press, 1969.

EVANS, K. M. *Planning Small-scale Research*. National Foundation for Educational Research, Slough, 1968.

GRIFFITHS, S. R. and DOWNES, L. W. *Educational Statistics for Beginners*. Methuen Educational, Education Paperbacks, 1969.

HANSON, E. L. and BROWN, G. A. *Starting Statistics*. Hulton Educational, 1969.

HOOPER, R. (ed.) *The Curriculum: Context, Design and Development*. Oliver & Boyd, 1971.

HUDSON, B. (ed.) *Assessment Techniques: an Introduction*. Methuen Educational, Education Paperbacks, 1973.

HUNTER, IAN M. L. *Memory*. Penguin Books, 1964.

JACKSON, S. *A Teacher's Guide to Tests and Testing*. Longmans Green, 1968.

KRATHWOHL, D. R., BLOOM, B. S., and MASIA, B. B. *Taxonomy of Educational Objectives: the Classification of Educational Goals*, Handbook II: Affective Domain. Longmans Green, 1964.

LADO, ROBERT. *Language Testing.* Longmans Green, 1961.

LEWIS, DAVID GARETH. *Statistical Methods in Education.* University of London Press, 1967.

MCINTOSH, D. M., WALKER, D. A., and MACKAY, D. *Scaling of Teachers' Marks and Estimates.* Oliver & Boyd, 1962.

MACINTOSH, H. G. (ed.) *Techniques and Problems of Assessment.* Edward Arnold, 1974.

MACINTOSH, H. G. and MORRISON, R. B. *Objective Testing.* University of London Press, 1969.

MARCUS, D. *Reports and Reporting.* Bosworth College, Desford, Leics., 1973.

MONTGOMERY, R. J. *Examinations: an Account of their Evolution as Administrative Devices in England.* Longmans Green, 1965.

NICHOLLS, A. and H. *Developing a Curriculum: a Practical Guide.* Allen & Unwin, 1972.

NISBET, J. D. and ENTWISTLE, N. J. *Educational Research Methods.* University of London Press, 1970.

NUTTALL, D. L. and WILLMOTT, A. S. *British Examinations: Techniques of Analysis.* National Foundation for Educational Research, Slough, 1972.

PIDGEON, D. A. 'The interpretation of test scores', *Educational Research*, **IV**, November 1961, 33–43.

RICHMOND, W. KENNETH. *The School Curriculum.* Methuen, Education Paperbacks, 1971.

ROSS, J. M., BUNTON, W. J., EVISON, P., and ROBERTSON, T. S. *A Critical Appraisal of Comprehensive Education.* National Foundation for Educational Research, Slough, 1972.

SCHOFIELD, H. *Assessment and Testing: an Introduction.* Unwin Educational, 1972.

THORNDIKE, ROBERT L. and HAGEN, ELIZABETH. *Measurement and Evaluation in Psychology and Education.* John Wiley, 1969.

VALETTE, REBECCA M. *Modern Language Testing: a Handbook.* Harcourt, Brace & World, 1967.

VERNON, PHILIP E. *Personality Assessment: a Critical Survey.* Methuen, Social Science Paperbacks, 1969.

VERNON, PHILIP E. *The Measurement of Abilities.* University of London Press, 1972.

WISEMAN, STEPHEN (ed.) *Examinations and English Education.* Manchester University Press, 1961.

WISEMAN, STEPHEN and PIDGEON, D. A. *Curriculum Evaluation.* National Foundation for Educational Research, Slough, 1970.

Schools Council publications

Examinations Bulletins
(The first four titles were published for the Secondary School Examinations Council whose work was taken over by the Schools Council.)

1. *The Certificate of Secondary Education: Some Suggestions for Teachers and Examiners.* HMSO, 1963.
2. *The Certificate of Secondary Education: Experimental Examinations – Mathematics.* HMSO, 1964.
3. *The Certificate of Secondary Education: an Introduction to Some Techniques of Examining.* HMSO, 1964.
4. *The Certificate of Secondary Education: an Introduction to Objective-type Examinations.* HMSO, 1964.
5. *The Certificate of Secondary Education: School-based Examinations: Examining, Assessing and Moderating by Teachers.* HMSO, 1965 (out of print).
6. *The Certificate of Secondary Education: Experimental Examinations – Technical Drawing.* HMSO, 1965.
7. *The Certificate of Secondary Education: Experimental Examinations – Mathematics 2.* HMSO, 1965.
8. *The Certificate of Secondary Education: Experimental Examinations – Science.* HMSO, 1965.
9. *The Certificate of Secondary Education: Trial Examinations: Home Economics.* HMSO, 1966.
10. *The Certificate of Secondary Education: Experimental Examinations: Music.* HMSO, 1966.
11. *The Certificate of Secondary Education: Trial Examinations – Oral English.* HMSO, 1966.
12. *Multiple Marking of English Compositions: an Account of an Experiment.* HMSO, 1966.
13. *The Certificate of Secondary Education: Trial Examinations: Handicraft.* HMSO, 1966.
14. *The Certificate of Secondary Education: Trial Examinations – Geography.* HMSO, 1966.
15. *Teachers' Experience of School-based Examining (English and Physics).* HMSO, 1967.
16. *The Certificate of Secondary Education: Trial Examinations: Written English.* HMSO, 1967.
17. *The Certificate of Secondary Education: Trial Examinations: Religious Knowledge.* HMSO, 1967.
18. *The Certificate of Secondary Education: the Place of the Personal Topic – History.* HMSO, 1968.

19. *CSE: Practical Work in Science.* Evans/Methuen Educational, 1969.
20. *CSE: a Group Study Approach to Research and Development.* Evans/Methuen Educational, 1970.
21. *CSE: an Experiment in the Oral Examining of Chemistry.* Evans/Methuen Educational, 1971.
22. *Question Banks: Their Use in School Examinations.* Evans/Methuen Educational, 1971.
23. *A Common System of Examining at 16+.* Evans/Methuen Educational, 1971.
24. *The Predictive Value of CSE Grades for Further Education.* Evans/Methuen Educational, 1972.
25. *CSE: Mode I Examinations in Mathematics: a Study of Current Practice.* Evans/Methuen Educational, 1972.
26. *Engineering Drawing at GCE A Level.* Evans/Methuen Educational, 1972.
27. *Assessment of Attainment in Sixth-form Science.* Evans/Methuen Educational, 1973.
28. *CSE: Two Research Studies.* Evans/Methuen Educational, 1974.
29. *Comparability of Standards between Subjects.* Evans/Methuen Educational, 1974.
30. *Comparability of Grade Standards in Mathematics at GCE A Level.* Evans/Methuen Educational, 1975.
31. *Continuous Assessment in the CSE: Opinion and Practice.* Evans/Methuen Educational, 1975.

Research Studies
Curriculum Evaluation Today: Trends and Implications edited by David Tawney. Macmillan Education, 1976.
Evaluation in Curriculum Development: Twelve Case Studies. Macmillan Education, 1973.
The Quality of Listening by Andrew Wilkinson, Leslie Stratta and Peter Dudley. Macmillan Education, 1974.

Teaching materials from curriculum development projects
Curriculum Design and Management in Geography: a Handbook for School Based Curriculum Renewal (Schools Council Geography 14–18 Project, Teacher's Handbook). Macmillan Education, 1976.

Index

189